Louis Comfort
Tiffany

Jacob Baal-Teshuva

Louis Comfort Tiffany

TASCHEN

KÖLN LONDON LOS ANGELES MADRID PARIS TOKYO

res

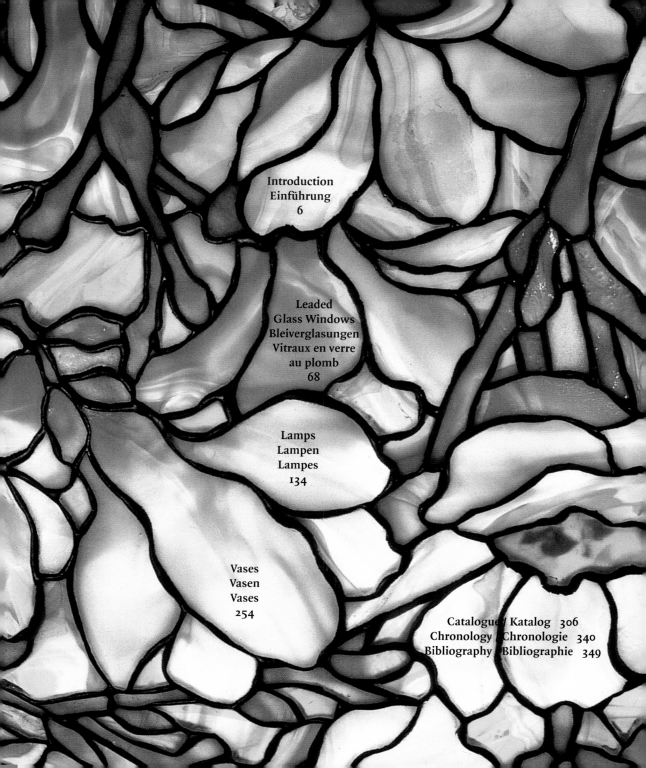

Introduction
Einführung

Tiffany. The man and his work

It is all a matter of education, and we shall never have good art in our homes until the people learn to distinguish the beautiful from the ugly. (Louis Comfort Tiffany)

Louis Comfort Tiffany (1848–1933) was the most important master of the decorative arts in America's "gilded age." He was a true visionary and one of the most original, creative, and influential designers of the period. Tiffany was the United States' leading proponent of Art Nouveau, the elegant, decorative and graceful style of ornamentation that flourished in Europe at the turn of the 20th century. He is also regarded as one of the first industrial designers to combine fine art and functional utility in his various creations, which are today known, appreciated and collected throughout the world. Tiffany was an industrious experimenter, obsessed with perfection and excellence, ideals he pursued to the fullest in his quest for a luxurious new aesthetic to suit American high style.

Tiffany's widely varied career stretched over more than half a century, from 1870 to the middle of the 1920's. He possessed natural talent in numerous artistic fields. Early in his career Tiffany proved to be a gifted painter, an aspect of his work that often escapes public attention. He was also an architect, designed both landscapes and interiors, and created new styles for furniture, draperies, wallpaper, and rugs. His pursuit of a unique vision led him to employ diverse materials including enamels, ornamental bronze, ceramics, silver, wood and wrought iron to produce everything from crucifixes and candelabrae to more prosaic items such as desk sets, clocks and picture frames.

But as exquisite as these objects are, Tiffany is known all over the world as America's premier glass artist. Glass was the medium in which he excelled, for the intrinsic beauty of the material opened limitless creative possibilities and permitted him the optimal realization of his aesthetic ideas. Under his direct supervision, the expert artisans in his studios produced thousands of stained glass windows and lamps, tableware, mosaics and the most magnificent glass jewelry.

It was of the utmost importance to Tiffany that every one of his creations be unique, and that each should bear

Tiffany. Der Mann und sein Werk

Es ist alles eine Frage der Bildung, und um sich mit guter Kunst umgeben zu können, müssen die Menschen lernen, das Schöne vom Hässlichen zu unterscheiden. (Louis Comfort Tiffany)

Louis Comfort Tiffany (1848–1933) war der bedeutendste Meister der dekorativen Künste im »goldenen Zeitalter« Amerikas. Er war ein wahrer Visionär und einer der originellsten, kreativsten und einflussreichsten Designer seiner Zeit. Tiffany war Führungsgestalt des Jugendstils in den Vereinigten Staaten schlechthin, des eleganten und anmutigen dekorativen Stils, der um die Wende zum 20. Jahrhundert in Europa seine Blütezeit erlebte. Er wird als einer der ersten Kunstindustrie-Designer betrachtet, der in seinen vielseitigen, in aller Welt bekannten, begehrten und gesammelten Schöpfungen Kunst und Funktionstüchtigkeit miteinander verband. Er war experimentierfreudig und besessen von dem Drang nach Perfektion und herausragender Leistung. So gelang ihm die Entwicklung einer neuen luxuriösen Ästhetik amerikanischen Stils, die höchsten Ansprüchen genügen sollte.

Tiffanys facettenreiche Karriere erstreckte sich über mehr als ein halbes Jahrhundert, von 1870 bis in die Mitte der 20er-Jahre des 20. Jahrhunderts. In vielen künstlerischen Bereichen war er ein Naturtalent. Zu Beginn seiner Laufbahn erwies er sich als ein begabter Maler – ein Aspekt seines Schaffens, der häufig übersehen wird. Er war Architekt, Innenarchitekt und Landschaftsgestalter. Zudem entwarf er Möbel, Stoffe, Tapeten und Teppiche. Immer auf der Suche nach einer neuen Vision, schuf er aus unterschiedlichen Materialien – Email, Bronze, Keramik, Silber, Holz und Schmiedeeisen – die verschiedensten Objekte: Kreuze und Kandelaber, aber auch Alltagsgegenstände wie Schreibtischgarnituren oder Bilderrahmen.

In aller Welt ist Tiffany aber vor allem als amerikanischer Glaskünstler bekannt. Die immanente Schönheit dieses Materials eröffnete ihm grenzenlose Gestaltungsmöglichkeiten, die es ihm gestatteten, seine ästhetischen Vorstellungen optimal umzusetzen. Unter seiner unmittelbaren Aufsicht brachten die besten Kunsthandwerker in seinen Studios Tausende von Buntglasfenstern sowie Lampen, Vasen, Tischdekorationen, Mosaiken und prachtvolle Schmuckstücke aus Glas hervor.

Tiffany : l'homme et l'œuvre

Tout est affaire d'éducation, et jamais nous n'aurons dans nos foyers un art de qualité tant que les gens n'auront pas appris à faire la différence entre le beau et le laid. (Louis Comfort Tiffany)

Louis Comfort Tiffany (1848–1933) fut le grand maître des arts décoratifs de l'« âge d'or » américain. Véritable visionnaire, il apparaît comme le designer le plus original, le plus inventif et le plus influent. Il fut aussi l'instigateur de l'Art Nouveau, style ornemental élégant, décoratif et gracieux qui s'épanouit en Europe au tournant du XXe siècle. Il est également considéré comme l'un des premiers designers industriels à allier sens artistique et utilité fonctionnelle dans ses diverses créations qui sont connues, appréciées et collectionnées aujourd'hui dans le monde entier. Tiffany fut un expérimentateur inlassable, habité par la perfection et le souci d'excellence dont il ne se départit jamais dans sa quête d'une nouvelle esthétique du luxe, adaptée aux exigences du style américain.

Sa carrière très diversifiée dura plus d'un demi-siècle, de 1870 jusque vers 1925. Il était doué de talents variés, dans diverses disciplines artistiques. D'abord, il se montra un peintre talentueux, un aspect de son œuvre souvent - négligé aujourd'hui. Puis il se fit architecte et conçut des espaces paysagers et des décors intérieurs, ainsi que de nouveaux styles de meubles, de draperies, de papiers peints et de tapis. Dans sa quête d'une vision unique, il fut amené à utiliser toutes sortes de matières telles que l'émail, le bronze ornemental, la céramique, l'argent, le bois et le fer forgé pour produire des objets très divers, des crucifix et des bougeoirs, ou plus prosaïques, des ensembles de bureau et encadrements de tableaux.

Bien que ces objets soient d'un goût exquis, Tiffany est mondialement connu comme le plus grand verrier américain. Le verre fut le moyen d'expression où il excella car la beauté intrinsèque du matériau lui offrit d'immenses possibilités créatives et lui permit la réalisation optimale de ses conceptions esthétiques. Sous sa supervision directe, dans ses propres ateliers, des artisans chevronnés produisirent des milliers de vitraux, de lampes, de services de table, de mosaïques et de merveilleuses joailleries, le tout en verre de couleur.

Pour Tiffany, il était essentiel que chacune de ses créations soit unique et porte le sceau de son style personnel.

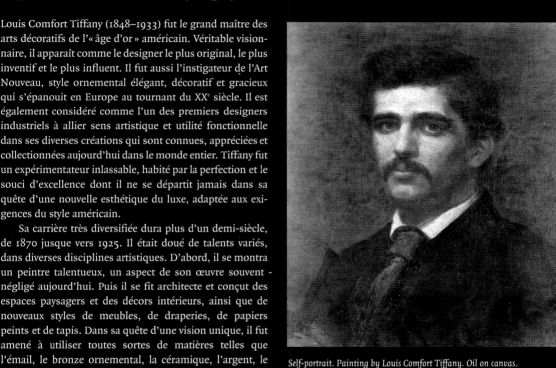

Self-portrait. Painting by Louis Comfort Tiffany. Oil on canvas.

Selbstporträt. Gemälde von Louis Comfort Tiffany. Öl auf Leinwand.

Autoportrait. Tableau de Louis Comfort Tiffany. Huile sur toile.

50.8 x 40.6 cm, c. 1872.
Collection of the National Academy of Design, NY.

PAGE/SEITE 6–7

"Louis Comfort Tiffany." Painting by Joaquín Sorolla y Bastida.
Oil on canvas.

»Louis Comfort Tiffany«. Gemälde von Joaquín Sorolla y Bastida.
Öl auf Leinwand.

« Louis Comfort Tiffany ». Tableau de Joaquín Sorolla y Bastida.
Huile sur toile.

155 x 225 cm, 1911. Coll. The Hispanic Society of America, NY.

he stamp of his individual style. He wanted to impart to his public the excitement of color and form that he personally enjoyed. He once asserted, "I have always striven to fix beauty in wood or stone, or glass or pottery, in oil or water-color, by using whatever seemed fittest for the expression of beauty; that has been my creed, and I see no reason to change it."

Even though most of his work was created to please late 19th-century tastes, Louis Comfort Tiffany was nevertheless the first American industrial artist to design in the spirit of the modern age. In contrast to Victorian design practices, he worked without rules, patterns or formulae. Tiffany's only (and seemingly endless) sources of inspiration were the beauty of the natural world and its spectrum of colors. He expressly discouraged imitation or copying: "God has given us our talents not to copy the talents of others, but rather to use our brains and our imagination in order to obtain the revelation of true beauty." A restless man, Tiffany applied his energy and vitality to a constant search for new technical inventions that would allow him to realize his artistic ideas. His versatility enabled him to become master of several media, and he demanded only the highest quality work from every department of his enterprise. His design legacy and imaginative virtuosity have gained him a permanent place as one of America's greatest creative geniuses.

Early life and painting career

"Nature is always right"—that is a saying we often hear from the past; and here is another: "Nature is always beautiful." (L. C. T.)

Louis Comfort Tiffany was born on February 18, 1848, the eldest son of Harriet and Charles Lewis Tiffany of New York City. C. L. Tiffany was the founder of Tiffany & Co., the most prestigious purveyor of jewelry, timepieces and silver objects in the world. Shortly after the company opened in 1837, the name of Tiffany became an international synonym for luxury, fine craftsmanship, good design and excellent taste. By 1870 its Fifth Avenue store was the place where presidents and royalty acquired the gifts they gave to visiting heads of state, with clients and recipients such as Queen Victoria of England, the czar of Russia and the khedive of Egypt. By 1900 Tiffany & Co. had over 1,000 employees

Tiffany legte größten Wert darauf, dass seine Schöpfungen einzigartig sind und den Stempel seines persönlichen künstlerischen Stils tragen. Er wollte der Welt die Freude an Farben und Formen vermitteln, die er selbst empfand: »Ich habe immer danach gestrebt, Schönheit festzuhalten, in Holz oder Stein, Glas oder Ton, Öl- oder Wasserfarbe, je nachdem, was mir jeweils am besten geeignet zu sein schien, Schönheit zum Ausdruck zu bringen; das war schon immer mein Credo, und ich sehe keinen Grund, davon abzuweichen.«

Auch wenn der größte Teil seines Werks auf den Geschmack des späten 19. Jahrhunderts abgestimmt war, handelte es sich bei Louis Comfort Tiffany um den ersten amerikanischen Designer, der im Geiste der Moderne arbeitete. Anders als die viktorianischen Designer folgte er mit seinen Entwürfen keinen Regeln oder Formeln. Seine einzige (und offenbar unerschöpfliche) Inspirationsquelle war die Schönheit der Welt der Natur mit ihrem reichen Farbenspektrum. Ausdrücklich wandte er sich gegen jede Form der Imitation: »Gott hat uns unsere Talente gegeben, damit wir mit Hilfe unseres Verstandes und unserer Phantasie wahre Schönheit erkennen und erreichen, nicht um das, was andere hervorgebracht haben, zu kopieren.« Rastlos widmete er seine ganze Energie und Vitalität der Suche nach technischen Innovationen, mit denen er seine künstlerischen Vorstellungen realisieren konnte. Dank seiner Vielseitigkeit erreichte er auf verschiedenen Gebieten große Meisterschaft und trieb seine Mitarbeiter in den einzelnen Abteilungen seiner Werkstatt zu immer neuen Höchstleistungen an. Sein gestalterisches Erbe und seine künstlerische Virtuosität sichern ihm einen festen Platz unter den größten kreativen Genies Amerikas.

Jugend und frühe Laufbahn als Maler

»Die Natur hat immer recht«, besagt eine alte Redensart, und ich möchte dem hinzufügen: »Die Natur ist immer schön.« (L. C. T.)

Louis Comfort Tiffany wurde am 18. Februar 1848 als ältester Sohn von Harriet und Charles Lewis Tiffany in New York City geboren. Charles Lewis Tiffany hatte 1837 in New York das Unternehmen Tiffany & Co. gegründet, das schon nach wenigen Jahren zum weltweit renommiertesten Lieferanten für Juwelen, Uhren und Silberwaren und zu einem

C. L. Tiffany

Charles Louis Tiffany, c. 1890.
Private collection

"Peonies." Painting by Louis Comfort
Tiffany. Oil on canvas.

»Pfingstrosen«. Gemälde von Louis Comfort
Tiffany. Öl auf Leinwand.

« Pivoines ». Tableau de Louis Comfort
Tiffany. Huile sur toile.

50.8 x 35.6 cm, c. 1920. Courtesy Dennis
Marchese & Co., Santa Barbara, CA.

its four branches located aroun
y's personal fortune stood at aro
g Louis was raised in an environm
esign; however, to his father's disa
ed no interest in joining the fam
announced that he would devote h
d pursue his own quest for beauty
862 to 1865 Tiffany attended the
ademy in Perth Amboy, New Jerse
Europe for the first time, touri
nce and Italy. In London he visited
Museum, whose extensive collecti
glass made a deep impression on
nuseum possesses a fine collecti
ny painted on site and documented
isited in sketches and photograp
eturn to New York he enrolled for
cademy of Design where, in 1867
ntings inspired by his European tra
lso at this time that he met the fa
cape painter George Inness (182
ormally with him, preferring to vi
dio rather than attend his cla
tonalist painter with early influen
udson River School, Inness instille
ppreciation of nature. Inness was
roup of French landscape painters
led in the village of Barbizon nea
vn as the Barbizon School, the gro
tant forerunners of Impressionism
aubigny, Theodore Rousseau, a
ss must have shared with his young
that "the purpose of the painter
n other minds the impression that
him. A work of art does not ap
does not appeal to the moral sens
ict, not to edify, but to awaken an
ly took this understanding of art to
desire to return to Europe was
n Paris, he briefly studied with th
er Léon-Charles-Adrien Bailly (1
care for his strict approach. In the
entalist salon painter Léon-Adolp

n aller Welt bekannten Synonym für Luxus, herausragende Qualität, gutes Design und exzellenten Geschmack wurde. Um 1870 hatte sich die Hauptniederlassung auf der Fifth Avenue als der Ort etabliert, wo Staatsoberhäupter wie Königin Victoria von England, der Zar von Russland und der Vizekönig von Ägypten die Kostbarkeiten erwarben, die bei Staatsbesuchen überreicht wurden. 1900 beschäftigte Tiffany & Co. in seinen insgesamt vier weltweiten Niederlassungen über 1000 Mitarbeiter, und Charles Lewis Tiffanys Privatvermögen wurde auf etwa 11 Mio. Dollar geschätzt. Der junge Louis wuchs in einer Welt des Luxus und des guten Geschmacks auf. Zur Enttäuschung seines Vaters zeigte er jedoch kein Interesse daran, in das Familienunternehmen einzutreten. Er wollte sich statt dessen den bildenden Künsten und seiner eigenen Suche nach Schönheit widmen.

Von 1862 bis 1865 besuchte Tiffany die Militärakademie Eagleswood in Perth Amboy, New Jersey. 1865 reiste er zum ersten Mal nach Europa. Die Reise führte ihn durch England, Irland, Frankreich und Italien. In London besuchte er das Victoria and Albert Museum mit seiner großartigen Sammlung römischer und syrischer Gläser, von der er zutiefst beeindruckt war. Heute besitzt dieses Museum auch eine prächtige Sammlung von Tiffany Gläsern. Tiffany hielt viele Stationen seiner Europareise auf Skizzen fest. Nach seiner Rückkehr nach New York schrieb

er sich für ein Jahr an der National Academy of Design en, wo er 1867 in seiner ersten Ausstellung Gemälde zeigte, die auf seine Europareise zurückgingen.

In dieser Zeit lernte er den berühmten amerikanischen Landschaftsmaler George Inness (1825–1894) kennen. Tiffany nahm lieber bei ihm privaten Malunterricht, als an den Kursen in der Akademie teilzunehmen. Inness, der unter dem Einfluss der romantischen Hudson River School zu malen begonnen hatte, weckte in Tiffany ein tiefes Interesse an der Natur. Er stand auch mit der Schule von Barbizon in Verbindung, einer Gruppe französischer Landschaftsmaler, zu der unter anderen Charles-François Daubigny, Théodore Rousseau und Camille Corot gehörten. Inness wird seinem jungen Schüler seine Philosophie vermittelt haben, die er wie folgt formulierte: »Der Maler hat einfach nur die Aufgabe, anderen Menschen genau den Eindruck zu vermitteln, den eine Szene auf ihn gemacht hat. Ein Kunstwerk spricht nicht den Intellekt, nicht den Sinn für Moral an. Es will nicht belehren, nicht erbauen, sondern eine Empfindung wachrufen.« Tiffany scheint sich dieses Kunstverständnis zu Herzen genommen zu haben.

Tiffanys Wunsch, nach Europa zurückzukehren, ging schon 1868 in Erfüllung. In Paris studierte er kurze Zeit bei dem Figurenmaler Léon-Charles Adrien Bailly (1826–1900), dessen Dogmatismus ihm jedoch nicht zusagte. Später, in den 1870er-Jahren, lernte er den Salonmaler Léon-Adolphe Auguste Belly (1827–1877) kennen, einen Vertreter des Orientalismus, der durch Darstellungen exotischer Kulturen und Orte bekannt geworden war. Bellys Gemälde übten einen starken Einfluss auf Tiffany aus, der sich in Paris zu einem der amerikanischen Tradition verhafteten Landschafts- und Genremaler entwickelte.

Zurück in New York, begegnete er 1870 im Century Club dem Künstler Samuel Colman (1832–1920), mit dem er sich anfreundete. Als sie sich im Jahr darauf in Granada trafen, reisten sie von dort aus zusammen nach Ägypten und Nordafrika. Unter dem Einfluss des damals sehr populären Orientalismus malte Tiffany in Marokko, Tunesien und Algerien Landschaften und Marktszenen – insbesondere in den Städten Tanger und Kairo –, manchmal dieselben Motive wie sein Reisegefährte Colman. Unter seinen Reisezielen scheint Nordafrika den größten Eindruck auf ihn gemacht zu haben; die Suks, die Landschaften und die exotischen Menschen in den Ländern des Maghreb schil

orientaliste Léon-Adolphe-Auguste Belly (1827–1877), célèbre pour ses descriptions de lieux et de civilisations exotiques. Ses tableaux évocateurs exercent une forte influence sur Tiffany, qui commence à s'imposer comme peintre de paysages et de genre, mais dans la tradition américaine et non française.

En 1870, quelque temps après son retour à New York, Tiffany fait la connaissance du peintre Samuel Colman (1832–1920) au Century Club. Très vite, ils deviennent amis. Un an plus tard, après avoir voyagé séparément à travers l'Europe, ils se retrouvent à Grenade et partent

ensemble pour l'Egypte et l'Afrique du Nord. Sous la forte influence de l'Orientalisme qui prévaut à l'époque, Tiffany peint des paysages et des scènes de marché au Maroc, en Tunisie et en Algérie, avec une prédilection pour les villes de Tanger et du Caire, en représentant parfois des sujets qui sont les mêmes que ceux de son compagnon de voyage. Il semble que l'Afrique du Nord l'ait particulièrement impressionné. Il excelle dans la peinture des souks, des paysages et de l'exotisme maghrébin. Au cours de ces voyages, il s'intéresse spécialement à l'art, à l'architecture

"Pushing Off the Boat, Sea Bright, New Jersey" (detail).
Painting by Louis Comfort Tiffany. Oil on canvas.

»Ablegemanöver in Sea Bright, New Jersey« (Ausschnitt).
Gemälde von Louis Comfort Tiffany. Öl auf Leinwand.

« Bateau sur la rive à Sea Bright, New Jersey » (détail).
Tableau de Louis Comfort Tiffany. Huile sur toile.

61 x 91 cm, 1887. Christie's Images.

Snake Charmer was exhibited at the 1876 Centennial Exhibition in Philadelphia along with other Tiffany paintings. Two years later, three of his paintings were shown at the Paris Exposition Universelle of 1878, including American street scenes like Duane Street, New York, in which he portrayed the everyday life of the great city. In Tin Peddler at Sea Bright, New Jersey, Tiffany depicted a small crowd gathered around a peddler selling his wares on the street. A self-portrait painted during this early period is in the collection of the National Academy of Design in New York. In addition to oils, Tiffany produced watercolors using the photographs he had taken in North Africa and in Europe as references. He continued to paint over the years, producing family scenes, views of the Hudson River, landscapes, and many cityscapes.

Tiffany had great ambition for his career as fine artist and participated in no fewer than 27 exhibitions in his young years. In 1870, at the tender age of 21, Tiffany was elected an associate member of the National Academy of Design in New York, as well as a member of the Century Club and of the American Watercolor Society. In 1877, Tiffany was a founding member of the Society of American Artists along

derte er mit großer Meisterschaft. Auf seinen Reisen entwickelte er ein starkes Interesse an der islamischen Kunst, Architektur und Ornamentik, das auf seiner Faszination für das romanische, maurische und japanische Kunsthandwerk aufbaute. In den Städten, die er bereiste, sammelte er Glas- und andere Objekte, die ihm später zweifellos als Inspirationsquelle dienten.

Tiffany hielt nicht nur viele der Orte, die er besuchte, in einem Skizzenbuch fest, sondern er machte auch Fotografien, die er später in seinem Atelier als Vorlagen für seine Gemälde verwendete. Auf einigen seiner erhalten gebliebenen Fotografien sind Menschen und Tiere – hauptsächlich Vögel – in Bewegung zu sehen: Zusammen mit Eadweard Muybridge (1830–1904) war Tiffany offenbar einer der ersten Künstler, die menschliche und tierische Bewegungsabläufe fotografierten.

Eines seiner bekanntesten Gemälde aus dieser Periode ist »Snake Charmer at Tangier« (»Schlangenbeschwörer in Tanger«; 1872, The Metropolitan Museum of Art, New York), das dem Betrachter die mystische und magische Atmosphäre dieser orientalischen Szene vermittelt. Und auch sein Gemälde »Market Day Outside the Walls of Tangier« (»Markttag vor den Mauern von Tanger«, 1873) führt dem Betrachter die orientalische Marktatmosphäre mit Hunderten von Arabern in ihren traditionellen Gewändern vor Augen. Als Kontrast dazu malte er 1874 in Genf eine elegante europäische Marktszene.

Zusammen mit anderen Tiffany-Gemälden wurde »Snake Charmer« 1876 auf der Weltausstellung in Philadelphia ausgestellt. Zwei Jahre später beteiligte sich Tiffany mit drei Gemälden an der Weltausstellung in Paris. Dazu gehörte auch die amerikanische Straßenszene »Duane Street, New York«, in der er die Atmosphäre des Alltagslebens in der Großstadt einzufangen wusste. »Tin Peddler at Sea Bright, New Jersey« zeigt eine kleine Menschenmenge um einen Hausierer, der seine Waren auf der Straße feilbietet. Tiffany malte in diesen Jahren Familienszenen, Ansichten vom Hudson River und viele andere Landschaften und Städte. Ein Selbstporträt aus der Zeit befindet sich in der Sammlung der National Academy of Design, New York. Neben Ölgemälden malte er auch Aquarelle, unter anderem nach seinen Fotografien aus Nordafrika und Europa.

Tiffany war ein ehrgeiziger Maler und nahm in seinen frühen Jahren an nicht weniger als 27 Ausstellungen teil.

et à l'ornementation islamiques, ce qui enrichit sa fascination pour les arts décoratifs romans, mauresques et japonais. Dans toutes les villes qu'il traverse, il collectionne des pièces de verre et autres objets, qui ne vont pas manquer de l'inspirer dans la conception de ses futures créations.

Si Tiffany consigne dans ses albums de croquis les différents lieux qu'il visite, il prend aussi des photos dont il va ensuite se servir, dans son atelier, pour documenter ses peintures. Dans celles qui nous sont parvenues, on voit des gens et des animaux, surtout des oiseaux, en mouvement. Comme Eadweard Muybridge (1830–1904), Tiffany semble avoir été l'un des premiers artistes à photographier des êtres vivants en mouvement.

Un de ses tableaux les plus connus de cette période, « Charmeur de serpents à Tanger », réalisé au cours de son voyage à Tanger en 1872, se trouve aujourd'hui dans la collection du Metropolitan Museum of Art de New York. Dans cette œuvre, il parvient à saisir, avec mystère et magie, l'étrange tradition orientale qui consiste à ensorceler un serpent, avec pour toile de fond une description précise de l'atmosphère locale. Dans une autre œuvre, intitulée « Marché ouvert hors les murs de Tanger », peinte en 1873, il réussit là aussi à saisir la fièvre du marché

"View From a Mosque." Painting by Louis Comfort Tiffany.
Oil on canvas.

»Blick von einer Moschee«. Gemälde von Louis Comfort Tiffany.
Öl auf Leinwand.

« Vue d'une mosquée ». Tableau de Louis Comfort Tiffany.
Huile sur toile.

33.4 x 29 cm, c. 1875. Christie's Images.

"Snake Charmer at Tangier." Painting by Louis Comfort Tiffany.
Oil on canvas.

»Schlangenbeschwörer in Tanger«. Gemälde von Louis Comfort Tiffany.
Öl auf Leinwand.

« Charmeur de serpents à Tanger ». Tableau de Louis Comfort Tiffany.
Huile sur toile.

69.9 x 97.8 cm, c. 1872.
Collection of The Metropolitan Museum of Art, NY. AKG, Berlin.

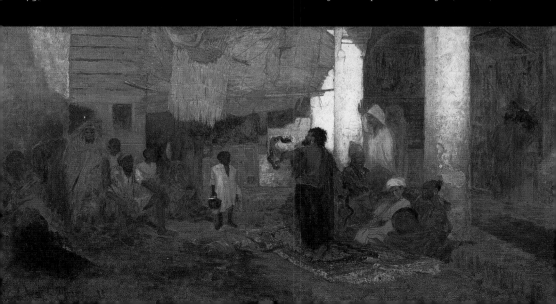

with artists such as John Singer Sargent, James McNeill Whistler, Thomas Eakins, Albert Pinkham Ryder and Augustus Saint-Gaudens. Tiffany became the group's first treasurer. He and the other members of this society were credited with having set new standards for modern American art at the time, and as a result, by 1880 Tiffany had become a full member of the National Academy of Design.

The public appreciated his paintings as works of fine art. Despite his modest success, Tiffany turned away from painting when he realized that his lack of academic training would not allow him the widespread adulation he craved and the personal wealth to which he had become accustomed. The sheer number of painters more skillful than he led him to seek out a less-crowded field where he could more easily make his mark. Tiffany's contribution to the development of American painting is hardly known, overshadowed by his fame as a glass artist. It was not until comparatively recently that Tiffany has been recognized as a truly important painter who, along with the other Society artists, gained wider recognition for American art. The retrospective of his paintings held in 1979 at the Grey Art Gallery at New York University gave the public a fresh opportunity to evaluate his work as a painter.

In describing his own paintings, Tiffany said they were "... one instant in time, a fragment of a happy day, nothing more." His accomplishments as a genre and landscape painter were of great use to him later as he designed stained glass window compositions that blended florals, landscapes and other natural elements. Tiffany's painting experience helped him to an intimate interpretation of his subject matter and a keen eye for the play of light and color. In a 1917 speech at the Rembrandt Club in Brooklyn, he mused: "When first I had a chance to travel in the East, and to paint where the people and the buildings also are clad in beautiful hues, the preeminence of color in the world was brought forcibly to my attention. I returned to New York wondering why we made so little use of our eyes, why we refrained so obstinately from taking advantage of color in our architecture and our clothing when Nature indicates its mastership."

Tiffany clearly felt that the Orient had much to teach the West about the appropriate use of color, since in his opinion, "our climate invites to sumptuous colors."

"Mrs. Hinkly Reading." Painting by Louis Comfort Tiffany. Oil on canvas.

»Porträt von Mrs. Hinkly, lesend«. Gemälde von Louis Comfort Tiffany. Öl auf Leinwand.

« Mme Hinkly lisant ». Tableau de Louis Comfort Tiffany. Huile sur toile.

66.5 x 51.2 cm, c. 1912.
Christie's Images.

870, im Alter von 21 Jahren, wurde Tiffany als außerordentliches Mitglied in die National Academy of Design in New York aufgenommen und zum Mitglied des Century-Clubs und der American Watercolor Society gewählt. 1877 gründete Tiffany zusammen mit Künstlern wie John Singer Sargent, James McNeill Whistler, Thomas Eakins, Albert Pinkham Ryder und Augustus Saint-Gaudens die Society of American Artists, deren erster Schatzmeister er wurde. Ihm und den anderen Mitgliedern dieser Gesellschaft wird das Verdienst zugeschrieben, in der modernen amerikanischen Kunst dieser Zeit neue Maßstäbe gesetzt zu haben. 1880 wurde Tiffany in Anerkennung seiner Leistungen zum Vollmitglied der National Academy of Design gewählt.

Tiffanys Gemälde wurden geschätzt und als Kunstwerke anerkannt. Dennoch gab er die Malerei auf, als er erkennen musste, dass er als Maler nicht die breite Anerkennung finden konnte, die er sich ersehnte und die ihm seinen gewohnten gehobenen Lebensstil gesichert hätte. Die stattliche Anzahl der handwerklich besser arbeitenden Maler seiner Zeit ließ ihn schließlich zu dem Entschluss kommen, sich auf einem anderen Gebiet zu profilieren, wo er sich nicht gegen so viel Konkurrenten behaupten musste. Da Tiffany vor allem als Glaskünstler berühmt geworden ist, ist sein Beitrag zur Entwicklung der amerikanischen Malerei weitgehend unbekannt geblieben. Erst in jüngerer Zeit findet Tiffany Anerkennung als bedeutender Maler, der zusammen mit anderen Künstlern der Society of American Artists der amerikanischen Malerei zu einer breiten öffentlichen Wertschätzung verhalf. Die Retrospektive seiner Gemälde, die 1979 in der Grey Art Gallery der New York University gezeigt wurde, gab dem Publikum Gelegenheit, sein malerisches Werk aus heutiger Sicht neu zu beurteilen.

Tiffany selbst beschrieb seine Gemälde einmal als »nichts weiter als Begebenheiten, Fragmente eines glücklichen Tages«. Seine Erfahrungen als Landschafts- und Genremaler waren ihm sehr hilfreich, als er später für seine Buntglasfenster Kompositionen entwarf, in denen er Landschaften, Blumen und andere Naturformen miteinander vermengte. Sie verhalfen ihm auch zu einer durchdachten Interpretation seiner Themen und zu einem genauen Blick für das Spiel von Licht und Farbe. In einer Rede, die er 1917 im Rembrandt-Club in Brooklyn hielt, sagte Tiffa-

nord-africain, faisant figurer des centaines d'Arabes en costume traditionnel. Vingt ans plus tard, Tiffany peint un autre marché, plus élégant, celui de Nuremberg, Allemagne, en contraste avec sa description des souks de Tanger.

Parmi d'autres œuvres, le « Charmeur de serpents » apparaît en 1876 à l'Exposition du Centenaire de Philadelphie. Deux ans plus tard, Tiffany présente trois tableaux à l'Exposition Universelle de Paris, parmi lesquels ses scènes de rues, comme « Duane Street, New York », où il parvient remarquablement à saisir la vie quotidienne de la ville. Dans « Le Ferblantier de Sea Bright, New Jersey » Tiffany montre une petite foule attroupée autour d'un colporteur qui vend sa marchandise aux passants. Il continue à peindre des scènes de famille, des vues de l'Hudson, des paysages et de nombreux sujets urbains. Un autoportrait de l'époque est conservé à National Academy of Design, à New York. Outre ses huiles, Tiffany réalise des aquarelles à partir des photographies prises en Afrique du Nord et en Europe.

Tiffany nourrit de grandes ambitions pour sa carrière d'artiste peintre et, au cours de ces premières années, participe à pas moins de vingt-sept expositions. En 1870, à peine âgé de 21 ans, il est élu membre associé de la National Academy of Design de New York, ainsi que membre du Century Club et de la Société américaine des Aquarellistes. En 1877, il est l'un des membres fondateurs de la Society of American Artists, en compagnie de personnalités telles que John Singer Sargent, James McNeill Whistler, Thomas Eakins, Albert Pinkham Ryder ou Augustus Saint-Gaudens. Tiffany devient le premier trésorier de ce groupe. Reconnu comme l'un des fondateurs, avec les autres membres de cette société, des nouveaux standards de l'art moderne américain, Tiffany devient membre à part entière de la National Academy of Design.

Le public aime ses peintures et les classe au rang des œuvres d'art. Malgré ce succès, Tiffany cesse de peindre au moment où il comprend que son manque de formation académique ne pourra pas lui permettre de jouir de l'adulation sans borne à laquelle il aspire, ni de l'aisance financière à laquelle il a toujours été habitué. Compte tenu du nombre de peintres plus doués que lui, il décide de se tourner vers un domaine moins encombré, où il pourra s'affirmer sans

"The Pyramids in Egypt." Painting by Louis Comfort Tiffany.
Oil on canvas.

»Die Pyramiden von Ägypten«. Gemälde von Louis Comfort Tiffany.
Öl auf Leinwand.

« Les pyramides d'Egypte ». Tableau de Louis Comfort Tiffany.
Huile sur toile.

51 x 76.2 cm, c. 1915.
Courtesy Dennis Marchese & Co., Santa Barbara, CA.

devote himself wholeheartedly to creating with glass, and
pursued with boundless energy his ambitious goal: the
translation of his talent and magnificent color sense into
environments designed for everyday living.

The founding of the firm

"... to bring beauty into your home
So you can live with it
And so enhance your life." (Louis Comfort Tiffany)

The United States enjoyed tremendous industrial and
commercial expansion during the 1870's and 1880's. With
this economic boom came a great demand for luxury items
from titans of industry and other wealthy families. Tiffany
not only possessed a unique artistic vision, he was also a
savvy businessman and had a natural marketing ability. In

...u reisen und dort die wunderbaren Farbtöne der Kleidung der Menschen und auch der Gebäude zu malen, wurde mir die überragende Bedeutung der Farbe in der Welt eindringlich bewusst. Ich kehrte nach New York zurück und wunderte mich, warum wir unsere Augen so vernachlässigen, warum wir uns so hartnäckig dem Gewinn bringenden Einsatz der Farbe in der Architektur und unserer Kleidung verschließen, wo doch die Natur uns die schönsten Beispiele zeigt.« Tiffany zufolge war es der Orient, der dem Okzident seit Menschengedenken ein Beispiel für den richtigen Umgang mit der Farbe gab, und er war überzeugt, dass »unser Klima nach üppigen Farben ruft«. Er gab die Malerei auf Leinwand und Karton zugunsten der Glasmalerei auf und setzte sich ein ehrgeiziges Ziel, das er mit grenzenloser Energie verfolgte: seine Begabung und seinen unübertrefflichen Sinn für Farbe in die Kreation von Objekten des Alltagslebens einzubringen.

Die Gründung der Firma

.. um Schönheit in Ihr Heim zu bringen, so dass Sie damit leben und Ihr Leben bereichern können. (Louis Comfort Tiffany)

In den 70er- und 80er-Jahren des 19. Jahrhunderts erlebten die Vereinigten Staaten eine große industrielle und kommerzielle Expansion. Der Wirtschaftsboom hatte unter den Industriemagnaten und anderen wohlhabenden Leuten eine steigende Nachfrage nach Luxusartikeln zur Folge. Tiffany war nicht nur ein begabter Künstler, sondern gleichzeitig auch ein hervorragender Geschäftsmann und ein großes Marketingtalent. Darüber hinaus konnte er auf dem guten Namen seines Vaters aufbauen. Zusammen mit drei Freunden – der Textilkünstlerin Candace Wheeler und den Malern Samuel Colman und Lockwood de Forest – gründete er 1879 eine auf Inneneinrichtungen spezialisierte Firma, die vier Jahre lang, bis 1883, bestehen sollte: Louis C. Tiffany & Associated Artists. Nach der Vorstellung des damals 27-jährigen Tiffany sollte das Unternehmen ein gewinnorientiertes »Geschäft« sein, kein philanthropisches oder sendungsbewusstes Unterfangen: »Es geht uns um das Geld, das mit Kunst zu machen ist, aber eben mit Kunst.«

Tiffany und seine Freunde lieferten nach neuen Entwürfen gestaltete Tapeten, Textilien und Möbel, die aus heimischen Materialien von amerikanischen Handwerkern...

il faudra attendre une période relativement récente pour qu'il soit reconnu comme un peintre d'importance qui, avec d'autres artistes de la Society, a donné ses lettres de noblesse à l'art américain. En 1979, une rétrospective de ses peintures, à la Grey Art Gallery de l'université de New York, fut l'occasion pour le public de réapprécier son œuvre de peintre.

Pour décrire ses peintures, Tiffany a dit qu'il s'agissait « d'un instant dans le temps, le fragment d'un jour heureux, rien de plus ». Ses talents de peintre de paysage et de genre vont se révéler fort utiles quand il conçoit ses vitraux où se mêlent paysages, compositions florales et autres éléments naturels. Son expérience picturale lui permet également une interprétation intime de son sujet et une perception aiguë des jeux de lumière et de couleurs. En 1917, au cours d'un discours au Rembrandt Club de Brooklyn, il déclare : « Quand je me suis rendu en Orient pour la première fois et que j'ai peint en ces lieux où les gens et les constructions sont revêtus de teintes magnifiques, mon attention a été frappée par la prééminence de la couleur dans le monde. Je suis rentré à New York en me demandant pourquoi nous, nous ne faisions que si peu usage de nos yeux, pourquoi nous nous retenions si obstinément d'user de la couleur dans notre architecture et nos vêtements quand la nature nous montre si clairement ses chef-d'œuvres. » Tiffany sent tout ce que l'Orient peut enseigner à l'Occident en matière d'utilisation de la couleur, car selon lui, « notre climat nous invite à utiliser des couleurs somptueuses. » Tiffany renonce alors à la peinture sur toile et sur bois pour se consacrer à la peinture au moyen du verre. Il met son immense énergie au service de sa grande ambition : l'expression de son talent et de son merveilleux sens de la couleur dans des environnements destinés à la vie quotidienne.

Création de la fabrique

... faire rentrer la beauté dans vos foyers pour vivre avec elle et en rehausser votre vie. (Louis Comfort Tiffany)

Entre 1870 et 1880, les Etats-Unis connaissent une grande expansion industrielle et commerciale. Ce boom économique s'accompagne d'une forte demande d'articles de...

addition, he was in a position to draw upon his father's reputation for quality goods.

Tiffany gathered three of his friends—textile designer Candace Wheeler and the painters William H. de Forest and Samuel Colman—and formed an interior design firm called L. C. Tiffany and Associated Artists. The company was in business for just four years, from 1879 to 1883. Tiffany, then 27 years old, stated that this endeavor would be a "business, not a philanthropy or amateur educational scheme. We are going after the money there is in art, but art is there, after all." The group provided original designs for wallpaper, textiles and furniture produced from local materials by American artisans. Most of the designs were created by Tiffany with themes of flowers and plants. Other were inspired by and adapted from Oriental, Indian, and Turkish carpets. Tiffany also drew on historical sources and exotic cultures such as those of Japan, China, Egypt, India, ancient Greece and the Islamic world.

He appreciated and was inspired by the craftsmanship of British designer William Morris (1834–1896) and others in the Arts and Crafts Movement that Morris founded. A writer and painter as well as a designer, Morris was one of the great social reformers of the Victorian period. He saw medieval handcraft traditions as the means to restore art to its rightful status as an integral part of human well-being, and believed that beauty could be found in objects of utility. In 1861 he founded the firm Morris, Marshall, Faulkner & Co. (called Morris & Co. from 1875) whose carvings, fabric, tapestries, wallpaper, stained glass and furniture are some of the finest examples of 19th century decorative art. Morris' credo was "Have nothing in your home that you do not know to be useful or believe to be beautiful." It is clear that Tiffany hoped to apply Morris' ideas to America's domestic interiors, but nature remained Tiffany's prime source of inspiration.

Tiffany was also a pioneer in the contemporary art movement now known as *Art Nouveau*, meaning "new art." The movement takes its title from the name of a Paris art gallery operated by Siegfried Bing, "L'Art Nouveau," which from 1895 to 1904 sought to infuse European fine and decorative arts with what he felt was a much-needed breath of fresh air. Bing (known as S. Bing) admired the artifacts produced by glass factories in Nancy, France, as well as art from Japan and, in America, Tiffany's creations

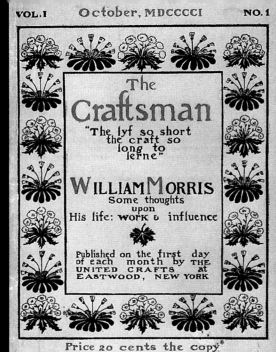

VOL. I   October, MDCCCCI   NO. 1

The Craftsman
"The lyf so short
the craft so
long to
lerne"

WILLIAM MORRIS
Some thoughts
upon
His life: work & influence

Published on the first day
of each month by THE
UNITED CRAFTS at
EASTWOOD, NEW YORK

Price 20 cents the copy

gefertigt wurden. Die meisten ihrer Entwürfe waren von Blumen- und Pflanzenformen inspiriert, andere von orientalischen, indischen und türkischen Teppichen. Tiffany griff auch auf historische Quellen aus dem Alten Griechenland und exotischen Ländern wie Japan, China, Ägypten, Indien sowie der islamischen Welt zurück. Seine wichtigste Inspirationsquelle blieb jedoch immer die Natur.

Auch von dem englischen Designer William Morris (1834–1896) und der von ihm initiierten Arts-and-Crafts-Bewegung ließ er sich inspirieren. Morris, Schriftsteller, Maler und Designer, war einer der großen viktorianischen Sozialreformer. Er wollte auf mittelalterliche Traditionen zurückgreifen, um die Kunst wieder zu einem integralen Bestandteil des menschlichen Lebens und Fortschritts werden zu lassen. Er war davon überzeugt, dass Schönheit in der Nützlichkeit zu finden sei. 1861 gründete er die Firma Morris, Marshall, Faulkner & Co. (seit 1875 Morris & Co.)

...xe chez les magnats de l'industrie et autres familles fortunées. Doué d'une vision artistique exceptionnelle, Tiffany possède aussi un formidable sens des affaires et du commerce. De plus, en matière de qualité, il peut s'appuyer sur la réputation de son père. Avec trois de ses amis, Candace Wheeler, dessinateur sur textile, et les peintres Samuel Colman et Lockwood de Forest, Tiffany crée une entreprise de décoration intérieure, la L. C. Tiffany and Associated Artists. Ils fonctionnent pendant quatre ans, de 1879 à 1883. Agé alors de 27 ans, Tiffany explique qu'il s'agit d'une affaire commerciale, et non d'un projet philanthropique ou éducatif. « Nous cherchons à gagner de l'argent en faisant de l'art, car l'art reste présent, après tout. »

Le groupe propose de nouveaux motifs de papiers peints, textiles et meubles, produits à partir de matériaux locaux et confiés à des artisans américains. La plupart des dessins sont élaborés par Tiffany, sur thèmes de fleurs et de plantes. D'autres s'inspirent de décors empruntés aux tapis orientaux, indiens et turcs. Tiffany puise aussi à la source de cultures historiques ou exotiques venues du Japon, de Chine, d'Egypte, d'Inde, de la Grèce antique et du monde islamique.

Il s'inspire aussi du dessinateur britannique William Morris (1834–1896), dont il admire la dextérité, ainsi que d'autres membres du groupe dit Arts and Crafts Movement (Arts et Artisanat) fondé par Morris. Ecrivain, peintre et décorateur, cet artiste fut l'un des grands réformateurs sociaux de l'Angleterre victorienne. Il voyait dans la tradition artisanale médiévale, le moyen de redonner à l'art son rôle dans l'épanouissement et le progrès des individus, et était persuadé que l'art pouvait trouver sa place dans les objets utilitaires. En 1861, il avait fondé la société Morris, Marshall, Faulkner & Co. (appelée Morris & Co. à partir de 1875) dont les bois sculptés, les tissus, les tapisseries, les vitraux, les meubles et les papiers peints demeurent parmi les plus beaux exemples de l'art décoratif du XIXe siècle. Selon Morris, « ne gardez rien chez vous dont vous ne connaissiez l'utilité ou dont vous n'admiriez la beauté. » De toute évidence, Tiffany cherche à appliquer les idées de Morris aux intérieurs américains, mais c'est la nature qui demeure néanmoins sa première source d'inspiration.

Tiffany joue aussi un rôle de pionnier dans le mouvement appelé de nos jours Art Nouveau, du nom d'une gale...

l'ART
NOUVEAU
BING

PARIS
22, RUE DE PROVENCE

Installations Modernes

MEUBLES, TENTURES, TAPIS, OBJETS D'ART

A l'Exposition Universelle de 1900, modèles de Meubles
vendus à tous les Musées d'Europe et hors d'Europe :
Londres, Berlin, Crefeld, Hambourg, Kaiserslautern,
Leipzig, Mulhouse, Nuremberg, Budapest, Gratz,
Lemberg, Vienne, Copenhague, Naples, St-Péters-
bourg, Helsingfors, Aarau, Berne, Drontheim,
Tokio, Musée des Arts décoratifs de Paris, etc.

'HORS CONCOURS, MEMBRE DU JURY

...he mit ihren Schnitzereien, Stoffen, Teppichen, Buntglasfenstern, Möbeln und Tapeten einige der schönsten Arte-
fakte dekorativer Kunst des 19. Jahrhunderts hervorbrach-
te. Sein Credo war: »Habe nichts in deinem Heim, was
nicht wirklich nützlich ist oder was du nicht für wirklich
schön hältst.« Tiffanys Vorstellung war es, Morris' Ideen
auf die amerikanischen Verhältnisse zu übertragen.

Tiffany war auch ein Pionier der Kunstbewegung, die
heute als Jugendstil bekannt ist. Die französische und eng-
lische Bezeichnung für den Jugendstil, Art Nouveau (»neue
Kunst«), geht auf die gleichnamige Pariser Galerie von
Siegfried Bing zurück, der von 1895 bis 1904 von dort aus
frischen Wind in die Kunst und das Kunstgewerbe Europas
bringen wollte. Bing bewunderte die Leistungen der Glas-
manufakturen von Nancy in Frankreich, die japanische
Kunst und die Arbeiten Tiffanys. Viele junge Künstler und
Designer lehnten sich damals gegen festgefahrene Traditionen auf, und unter verschiedenen Namen setzte sich
der neue Stil in ganz Europa durch. In Österreich war er als
Sezessionsstil bekannt, in Italien als stile liberty oder stile
floreale, in Spanien als modernismo und in Frankreich auch
als style métro (nach Hector Guimards Metallentwürfen für
die Eingangstore der Pariser Metrostationen). Bing vertrat
in seiner Galerie die besten dieser Künstler: Emile Gallé,
Koloman Moser, Alfons Maria Mucha, René Lalique, Louis
Majorelle, Hector Guimard, Josef Hoffmann, Charles Rennie Mackintosh, William Morris, Henri van de Velde und
den Katalanen Antonio Gaudí sowie Tiffany. Bing setzte
sich in seiner Galerie auch für innovative Künstler wie Félix
Vallotton und Edvard Munch ein.

Verschiedene Jugendstilkünstler und -architekten –
zum Beispiel Hector Guimard – arbeiteten mit aus der
Natur abgeleiteten abstrakten Formen. Tiffany dagegen
verwarf solche Abstraktionen zugunsten einer traditionel-
leren Wiedergabe der Schönheit der Natur. Tiffany, der in
der Blütezeit des Jugendstils regelmäßig nach Europa reiste, war mit den Zielsetzungen der Bewegung bestens ver-
traut und wusste sie in New York seinen eigenen Vorstellungen gemäß umzusetzen.

1882 wurde Tiffanys Firma vom amerikanischen Präsidenten Chester A. Arthur beauftragt, Teile des Weißen
Hauses in Washington, D.C., neu einzurichten. Arthur
stammte aus New York und kannte und bewunderte
Tiffanys Arbeit. Tiffany fertigte für das Weiße Haus einen...

...ie parisienne, dirigée par Siegfried Bing, qui, entre 1895
et 1904, avait tenté d'insuffler dans les beaux-arts et les
arts décoratifs européens ce qu'il considérait comme une
bouffée d'air frais fort nécessaire. Bing (appelé S. Bing)
professait une grande admiration pour les verreries de
Nancy, et pour celles de l'art japonais, et en Amérique
pour le travail de Tiffany lui-même. Dans toute l'Europe, de
jeunes artistes et créateurs se rebellaient contre l'étouffe-
ment et la banalité de certaines traditions artistiques, et
chaque pays donnait un nom à ce mouvement : le Jugendstil en Allemagne, le style Sécession en Autriche, le Stile
Liberty ou Stile Floreale en Italie, le Modernismo en Es-
pagne et le style Métro en France (en hommage aux fer-
ronneries originales qui décoraient les entrées du nouveau
métro de Paris, dues à Hector Guimard). La galerie de S.
Bing présentait les meilleurs d'entre eux, parmi lesquels
Emile Gallé, Koloman Moser, Alfons Maria Mucha, René
Lalique, Louis Majorelle, Hector Guimard, Josef Hoffman,
Charles Rennie Mackintosh, William Morris, Henri van de
Velde et le catalan Antoni Gaudí, sans oublier Tiffany lui-
même. Bing vendait aussi des tableaux signés par des ar-
tistes novateurs tels que Félix Vallotton ou Edvard Munch.

Plusieurs artistes et architectes Art Nouveau, comme
Hector Guimard, utilisaient dans leurs œuvres des formes
abstraites dérivées de la nature. Mais Tiffany rejette cette
sorte d'abstraction et préfère reproduire la beauté de la
nature de façon plus traditionnelle. Il passe dix années à
voyager entre l'Europe et les Etats-Unis, au moment où
l'Art Nouveau connaît sa plus grande popularité. Il en comprend parfaitement les objectifs et contribue à leur donner
forme en accord avec ses propres aspirations artistiques.

En 1882, la fabrique Tiffany reçoit une importante com-
mande du Président des Etats-Unis, Chester A. Arthur. Il
s'agit de refaire la décoration de certaines sections de la
Maison Blanche. Le président, d'origine new-yorkaise, est
un connaisseur et grand admirateur de l'œuvre de Tiffany.
L'artiste réalise alors un grand écran en verre, à trois pans,
destiné à séparer les domaines privés et publics de la Maison
Blanche, ainsi que plusieurs appliques murales en miroir.
Malheureusement, à peine vingt ans plus tard, le président
Theodore Roosevelt fera redécorer la Maison Blanche, dans
l'élégance et la simplicité du néoclassique. Les verreries de
Tiffany sont alors retirées et on obéit au président qui or-
donne de « briser cet écran en mille morceaux ».

he Neoclassical style of simple elegance. He had Tiffany's glass decorations removed and later destroyed at his express order: "Break that Tiffany screen into small pieces."

In addition to the presidential commission, throughout the 1880's and into the 1890's Tiffany and his associates decorated the homes of many of the wealthiest and most prominent families in America, including those of Andrew Carnegie, Henry Osborne Havemeyer, John Taylor Johnston (then president of the Metropolitan Museum of Art), Cornelius Vanderbilt II, and the writer Mark Twain. Havemeyer accumulated a large collection of Tiffany glass that he later donated to the Metropolitan Museum of Art in New York.

In 1883 L.C. Tiffany & Associated Artists disbanded, in large part because Tiffany had become increasingly interested in working almost exclusively with glass. The breakup was friendly, and the other two members went on to pursue independent projects. Tiffany was free to accept design projects on his own and did so, but increasingly he focused his energies on developing new ways to further his goal of infusing the world with the color he so loved.

Tiffany's glass windows: Light upon color

Make a material in which colors and combinations of colors, shades, hues, tints and tones [are] there without surface treatment as far as possible. (L. C. T.)

Tiffany was very much intrigued by the colored glass he saw on his many trips to Europe and the North Africa. As a colorist, he was also deeply impressed by examples of old Syrian and Roman glass that had become iridescent after centuries of contact with minerals in the soil in which they had been buried.

The earliest glass in history was Egyptian in origin, with technically advanced examples dated by historians to 1450 BC. The technique of glassblowing with a hollow pipe was invented in Syria in the 1st century BC, and later perfected by the Romans. Glass is even mentioned in the Bible: "But where shall wisdom be found? And where is the place of understanding? ... It cannot be valued in the gold of Ophir, in precious onyx or sapphire. Gold and glass cannot equal it, nor can it be exchanged for vessels of fine gold." (Job 28:12, 16–17) It is important to note that glass is mentioned along with gold, precious stones, and

sein großen drehenden Glasparavent, der die öffentlichen von den privaten Räumen trennte, sowie mehrere Wandleuchten und Wandspiegel. Leider ordnete Präsident Theodore Roosevelt nur 20 Jahre später eine neue, von schlichter Eleganz geprägte Innenausstattung im neoklassizistischen Stil an. Tiffanys Glasdekorationen wurden entfernt und auf ausdrücklichen Wunsch des Präsidenten zerstört: »Haut diesen Tiffany-Paravent in tausend Stücke.«

Auch die bekanntesten und reichsten amerikanischen Familien ließen ihre Häuser von Tiffany und seinen Geschäftspartnern ausstatten: die Großindustriellen Andrew Carnegie, Cornelius Vanderbilt II und Henry Osborne Havemeyer, John Taylor Johnston, der Präsident des Metropolitan Museum of Art in New York, und der Schriftsteller Mark Twain, um nur einige zu nennen. Henry Osborne Havemeyer sammelte zahlreiche Tiffany-Gläser, die er später dem Metropolitan Museum of Art schenkte.

1883 wurde Louis C. Tiffany & Associated Artists aufgelöst, hauptsächlich weil Tiffany selbst sich auf die Beschäftigung mit Glas zu konzentrieren begonnen hatte. Die Trennung erfolgte in freundschaftlichem Geist, und seine Partner gingen eigene Wege. Tiffany führte zwar noch einige Ausstattungsaufträge aus, doch mehr und mehr wandte er sich der Suche nach neuen Möglichkeiten zu, der Welt die denkbar schönsten Farben zu schenken.

Licht auf Farbe: Tiffanys Glasfenster

Ein Material, welches Farben und Farbkombinationen, Schattierungen, Farbtöne und Nuancen so weit wie möglich ohne Oberflächenbehandlung enthält. (L. C. T.)

Tiffany war fasziniert von den farbigen Gläsern, die er auf seinen Reisen durch Europa und Nordafrika gesehen hatte. Als Kolorist war er auch tief beeindruckt von den Gläsern der alten Syrer und Römer, die jahrhundertelang im Erdboden gelegen und durch den Kontakt mit Mineralien einen irisierenden Glanz bekommen hatten.

Die frühesten bekannten Gläser stammen aus Ägypten. Die ersten technisch anspruchsvollen Exemplare werden auf etwa 1450 v. Chr. datiert. Die Technik des Glasblasens mit Hilfe einer Glasmacherpfeife wurde im 1. Jahrhundert v. Chr. in Syrien erfunden und später von den Römern perfektioniert. In der Bibel wird bereits Glas erwähnt: »Di

Outre la commande présidentielle, Tiffany et ses associés décorent les maisons des familles les plus riches et les plus célèbres comme celles de Andrew Carnegie, Cornelius Vanderbilt II, Henry Osborne Havemeyer, John Taylor Johnson (président du Metropolitan Museum of Art), ou de l'écrivain Mark Twain. Havemeyer rassemble une importante collection de verres de Tiffany, dont il fera don au Metropolitan Museum of Art de New York.

En 1883, L. C. Tiffany & Associated Artists se séparent, surtout parce que Tiffany s'intéresse désormais presque exclusivement au verre. La rupture est amicale et les deux autres continuent de poursuivre, indépendamment, leurs projets. Tiffany peut maintenant se consacrer librement aux siens et propager, dans le monde entier, ces couleurs qu'il aime tant.

Lumière sur couleur : les vitraux Tiffany

Créer un matériau dans lequel les couleurs, avec leurs combinaisons, leurs nuances, leurs teintes et leurs tonalités sont présentes sans, si possible, le moindre traitement de surface. (L. C. T.)

Tiffany avait été fort intrigué par les verres de couleur découverts au cours de ses voyages en Europe et au Proche-Orient. Grand coloriste, il avait aussi été fort impressionné par d'antiques verres syriens et romains, devenus irides-

WILLIAM WATERS, *Architect*   CORNER OF A LIVING ROOM   *Executed by* TIFFANY STUDIOS

THE WELL-APPOINTED HOME

is always regarded as an indubitable mark of taste and refinement. The TIFFANY STUDIOS have unusual facilities for planning and executing INTERIOR DECORATIONS, SPECIAL LIGHTING FIXTURES and FURNISHINGS and cordially invite an inspection of their DISTINCTIVE SERVICE, which consists of submitting colored sketches of a complete decorative scheme as well as samples of the HANGINGS, RUGS, FURNITURE and FIXTURES, so that one may see the effect produced and know the cost of same before any order is given or obligation incurred.

TIFFANY ⑤ STUDIOS

347-355 MADISON AVE.   COR.45TH ST.NEW YORK CITY.
CHICAGO OFFICE,ORCHESTRA BVILDING - BOSTON OFFICE,LAWRENCE BVILDING.

Detail of a 13th-century stained glass window, Cathedral of Notre Dame, Paris.

Detail eines Buntglasfensters aus dem 13. Jahrhundert in der Kathedrale Notre Dame in Paris.

Détail d'un vitrail du XIIIᵉ siècle dans la cathédrale Notre-Dame de Paris.

Private collection.

other materials of great value. And of all these treasures glass is the only material made by human hands. Tiffany clearly appreciated the implications of this fact.

Tiffany was also deeply impressed by Europe's Gothic cathedrals with their myriad and spectacular stained glass windows. Later, in a 1917 speech to the Rembrandt Club in Brooklyn, he said: "Naturally, I was attracted to the old glass windows of the 12th and 13th centuries, which have always seemed to me the finest ever." The art of stained glass originated in Byzantium in the 4th to 6th centuries and reached its creative peak in Western Europe. The oldest completely intact stained glass windows are found in the Augsburg Cathedral in Germany, which dates to about 1050–1150. This form of expression makes exceptional demands on the artist who creates its design, and also requires specially trained artisans to bring it to life. Tiffany would eventually have access to both.

However, as much as Tiffany admired the coloration of medieval glass, he was convinced that the quality of contemporary glass could be improved upon. In his own words, the "rich tones are due in part to the use of poor metal full of impurities, and in part to the uneven thickness of the glass, but still more because the glass maker of that day abstained from the use of paint." Tiffany did not like the contemporary technique of painting onto the glass, which he felt obscured and disturbed the natural transparency of glass. Instead, he wanted the glass itself to transmit texture and rich colors, and he spent much of his life experimenting to find a means to duplicate—and eventually greatly exceed—the effect of the medieval stained glass he so admired. Tiffany's respect for the innate properties of glass led him to his greatest innovation—the development of a type of glass he called Favrile.

The word *favrile* is derived from the Latin word *fabrilis*, meaning made by hand. Favrile glass is produced by exposing molten glass to a series of fumes and metallic oxides that infuse it with glowing colors and an exciting iridescence. In 1880 Tiffany applied to the U.S. Patent Office, and with patent number 837418, dated February 8, 1881, was granted his first patent for Favrile glass. In that year he registered three patents having to do with the production and coloring of glass. In an 1880 letter of application for one of those patents he wrote: "Be it known that I, Louis C. Tiffany, a citizen of the United States, residing

veisnen aber, wo ist sie zu finden, und wo ist der Ort der
Einsicht? ... Nicht wiegt sie Gold aus Ofir auf, kein kost-
barer Karneol, kein Saphir. Gold und Glas stehen ihr nicht
gleich, und reinstes Gold wiegt sie nicht auf.« (Hiob 28,12,
16–17).

Glas wird also in der Bibel mit Gold, kostbaren Edelsteinen und anderen wertvollen Materialien in einem Atem-
zug genannt. Von allen diesen Kostbarkeiten ist Glas jedoch das einzige künstlich hergestellte Material, und dieser Gedanke wird für Tiffany ein Ansporn gewesen sein.

Auch von den gotischen Kathedralen Europas mit ihren
zahllosen Buntglasfenstern war Tiffany zutiefst beeindruckt. In einer 1917 im Rembrandt-Club in Brooklyn gehaltenen Rede sagte er: »Natürlich fühlte ich mich zu den
alten Glasfenstern aus dem 12. und 13. Jahrhundert hinge-
zogen, die für mich die schönsten überhaupt geblieben
sind.« Die Kunst der Glasmalerei hatte ihren Ursprung im
4. bis 6. Jahrhundert in Byzanz und erreichte ihre Blütezeit
mit der gotischen Architektur in Westeuropa. Die ältesten
vollständig erhaltenen gotischen Buntglasfenster sind die
des Augsburger Doms (ca. 1050–1150). Die Kunst der Glasmalerei stellt sowohl an den für den Entwurf verantwort-
lichen Künstler als auch an den mit der Ausführung betrau-
en Kunsthandwerker besonders hohe Ansprüche. Tiffany
brachte es in beiden Bereichen zu großer Meisterschaft.

Tiffany bewunderte die farbenfrohen Buntglasfenster
aus dem Mittelalter: »Ihre reichen Farben haben ihre Ursa-
che teils in der Verwendung einer mit Verunreinigungen an-
gefüllten Schmelzmasse, teils in der ungleichmäßigen Di-
cke des Glases, vor allem sind sie jedoch damit zu erklären,
dass die Glasmacher jener Zeit keine Farben verwendeten.«
Einen großen Teil seines Lebens widmete Tiffany der
Suche nach Möglichkeiten, die Qualität dieses farbigen
Glases zu erreichen oder gar zu übertrumpfen. Im 19. Jahrhundert war es üblich geworden, die Glasoberfläche zu bemalen, was die natürliche Transparenz des Materials beein-
trächtigte. Tiffany wollte stattdessen ein Glas entwickeln,
das selbst, ohne äußere Behandlung, eine ansprechende
Textur und satte Farben zeigte. Und seine Experimente waren schließlich von Erfolg gekrönt. Mit der Entwicklung
einer Glassorte, die er »Favrile« nannte, gelang ihm seine
bedeutendste Erfindung.

Der Begriff »Favrile« leitet sich vom Lateinischen »fa-
rilis« »handgemacht« ab. Indem heißes Glas verschiede-

En Europe, il avait été aussi très impressionné par les
cathédrales gothiques, et leurs milliers de vitraux. En 1917
lors d'un discours au Rembrandt Club de Brooklyn, il explique : « Naturellement, je me suis senti particulièrement
attiré par les vitraux des XIIe et XIIIe siècles, qui m'ont
toujours semblé les plus beaux du monde. » L'art du vitrail
naquit dans la Byzance des IVe et VIe siècles, avant d'atteindre son apogée en Europe occidentale. Les plus anciens vitraux intégralement conservés se trouvent dans la
cathédrale d'Augsbourg en Allemagne, et remontent à 1050-
1150. Si cette forme d'expression exige de son créateur des
qualités exceptionnelles, sa réalisation demande aussi des
artisans fort spécialisés. Tiffany va s'efforcer de répondre
à cette double exigence.

Pour grand admirateur qu'il soit des colorations du
verre médiéval, Tiffany émet quelques réserves quant à la
qualité de la production d'alors. Il déclare : « La richesse des
tons est due en partie à l'utilisation de métal de creuset
plein d'impuretés, en partie à l'épaisseur irrégulière du
verre, mais surtout au fait que le verrier de l'époque s'est
bien gardé d'utiliser de la peinture. » Tiffany va passer une
grande partie de sa vie à trouver le moyen de reproduire
voire d'améliorer l'effet tant admiré. Il n'aime guère la
technique d'alors qui consiste à peindre sur le verre. Pour
lui, cela obscurcit et perturbe la transparence naturelle du
verre. Il préfère que le verre révèle sa texture et la richesse de
ses nuances. C'est ce respect pour le verre qui va le mener à sa
plus grande découverte : ce verre qu'il nomme Favrile.

Le terme « favrile » vient du latin « fabrilis » qui signifie
fabriqué à la main. Il se produit en exposant le verre à
haute température à une série de vapeurs et d'oxydes métalliques, ce qui lui confère un aspect irisé et un chatoie-
ment extraordinaires. Tiffany fait enregistrer sa découverte au Bureau des Brevets Américains, sous le numéro
837 418 le 8 février 1881, sous le nom de brevet Favrile. En
1879, il avait déjà obtenu le brevet opalin. A partir de 1881
il dépose trois autres brevets concernant la production et la
coloration du verre, dont un pour le verre opalin. En 1880
dans une lettre accompagnant l'une de ses demandes de
brevet, il écrit :

« Je soussigné Louis C. Tiffany, citoyen des Etats-Unis,
résident de la ville du Comté et de l'Etat de New York,
déclare avoir inventé pour la fabrication de vitraux, des
améliorations nouvelles et utiles dont les spécifications

in the city, county and state of New York, have invented new and useful improvements in colored glass windows [that introduce] a new character of glass in colored glass windows. [...] The improvement consists in a metallic luster being given to one surface of pieces of glass and the insertion of such glass among other pieces of colored glass in a window or mosaic. The effect is a highly iridescent one and of pleasing metallic luster [...] The metallic luster is produced by forming a film of a metal or its oxide, or a compound of a metal, on or in the glass either by exposing it to vapors or gases or by direct application. It may also be produced by corroding the surface of the glass, such processes being well known to glass manufacturers ... all glass windows are, by the application of this metallic luster, made more beautiful in effect, at night, producing a highly iridescent and more lustrous effect ... "

In 1892 Tiffany opened a new glass factory in Corona, New York, where he continued research and development designed to further improve his glass. He used standard metallic oxides such as chromium, silver, gold, cobalt and even uranium in various combinations to achieve the desired translucency. Tiffany claimed that it took him 30 years to learn the art of glassmaking, despite the scoffing of his co-workers, who did not believe it could work. His trademark application for the name Favrile, as applied to his own glass, was approved in 1894.

Favrile glass was a major breakthrough for Tiffany, to his mind surpassing even the best of the 13th-century glasswork. He used Favrile glass with its haunting iridescent colors in all his windows, lamps, vases, and mosaics. Although iridescent glass had been produced earlier in the 19th century by Pantin in France, Edward Webb in England, and Lobmeyer in Austria, it was only when Tiffany, and later J. Loetz in Bohemia, began to market it widely through S. Bing's Paris art gallery that it became truly popular. According to experts, Favrile glass also served as an emancipation for the art of creating pieced glass windows. It opened possibilities both pictorially and decoratively, pictorially because of the limitless atmospheric effects one can achieve with it, and decoratively because of the intrinsic beauty of the material. In fact, Favrile glass was admired for its delicacy, and was described in contemporary literature as resembling "wings of butterflies and peacocks with their magic colors."

es intensive Farben mit einer faszinierenden Irisierung an. Am 8. Februar 1881 wurde Tiffanys irisierendes Favrile-Glas unter der Patent-Nr. 837 418 vom United States Patent Office patentiert. 1881 wurden Tiffany drei Patente auf Methoden zur Herstellung und Einfärbung von Glas bewilligt, von denen eines ebenfalls die Opaleszentglastechnik betraf. In einem 1880 eingereichten Antrag für eines dieser Patente schrieb er: »Hiermit sei bekannt gegeben, dass ich, Louis C. Tiffany, Bürger der Vereinigten Staaten, wohnhaft in der Stadt, im Bezirk und im Staat New York, neue und nützliche Verbesserungen im Bereich der Fertigung von Buntglasfenstern erfunden habe, die im Folgenden spezifiziert werden. Diese Erfindung bezieht sich auf die Einführung eines neuartigen Glases für Buntglasfenster … Bei der Verbesserung handelt es sich um einen metallischen Glanz, womit die Glasstücke auf einer Oberfläche versehen werden, und um die Einfügung solchen Glases zwischen andere Stücke gefärbten Glases in einem Fenster oder Mosaik. Dies ergibt einen äußerst irisierenden Effekt mit einem

type de verre pour les vitraux … L'amélioration consiste à appliquer un lustre métallique sur une surface de morceaux de verre, et à insérer ce verre parmi d'autres morceaux de verre de couleur, dans un vitrail ou une mosaïque. Il en résulte un effet d'irisation avec un joli lustre métallique, variant d'un morceau à l'autre, selon la direction du regard et l'éclat de la lumière qui tombe directement sur le verre ou le transperce. … Le lustre métallique est produit par le dépôt d'un métal, de son oxyde, ou d'un composé de métal, sur ou dans le verre, par exposition à des vapeurs ou à des gaz, ou par application directe. Ce lustre peut aussi être produit par corrosion de la surface du verre. Tous ces procédés de corrosion sont bien connus des fabricants … Grâce à l'application de ce brillant métallique, tous les vitraux se trouvent embellis, dans l'obscurité, et produisent un effet plus brillant et plus irisé, et, une fois placés sur une surface de verre opalin, en font disparaître la monotonie de la blancheur et l'apparence piquetée … »

Tiffany had a strong adversary and competitor in the glass business in the person of John La Farge (1835–1910), who, like Tiffany, was a painter as well as a decorative artist. But he was not Tiffany's only competition: 65 other interior design firms were in operation at the time in New York, most of which worked with glass to some degree. Tiffany and La Farge were the designers who truly revolutionized the art of stained glass in the late 1870's. Prior to that time, window production had been poor in quality and unchanged since medieval times—glass was painted or stained rather than producing its color effects from within the material itself. Both Tiffany and La Farge achieved, each in his own way, a greater density of glass and more intensity of color. There is no doubt that La Farge's work had an influence on Tiffany and helped spur some of his technical innovations.

One of those innovations was glass plating, that is, layering one or more sheets of glass in order to achieve greater depth of color and, at times, a three-dimensional effect. Tiffany was able to select glass from his own stock of thousands of different-colored sheets, giving him a distinct advantage over his competitors, who habitually used the limited range of commercially available glass sheets. Tiffany hired the best-known glassblowers and chemists, drawing them from both Italy and England with very high salaries, in order to develop the colors and textures he envisioned. By 1895 he had created all the glass varieties he needed and was no longer purchasing sheet glass. In his address to the Rembrandt Club in 1917 Tiffany stated: "By the aid of studies in chemistry and through years of experiments, I have found means to avoid the use of paints, etching or burning, or otherwise treating the surface of the glass so that now it is possible to produce figures in glass of which even the flesh tones are not superficially treated, but built up of what I call 'genuine glass' because there are no tricks of the glass maker needed to express flesh."

In addition to this technical disadvantage, La Farge found it difficult to compete for clients against Tiffany, whose family connections through Tiffany & Co. put him in close, regular contact with precisely those people who were in a position to commission work. Tiffany was able to utilize his superior marketing ability, keen business sense, and connections to the world's rich and famous to tap into

nach Perspektive und Brillanz oder Stumpfheit des Glases durch das hindurchschimmernde Licht ständig ändert. ..
Der metallische Glanz wird hervorgerufen, indem auf oder in dem Glas ein Film eines Metalls oder seines Oxids oder einer Metallverbindung erzeugt wird, entweder durch direktes Auftragen oder indem das Glas Dämpfen oder Gasen ausgesetzt oder die Oberfläche des Glases korrodiert wird. Alle diese Prozesse sind den Glasherstellern geläufig ..
Durch die Anwendung dieses metallischen Glanzes erhalten alle Glasfenster nachts eine schönere, ungemein irisierende und strahlende Wirkung, und auf einer Opaleszentglasoberfläche werden auf diese Weise die stumpfe Blässe und das fleckige Erscheinungsbild beseitigt.«

1892 eröffnete Tiffany in Corona auf Long Island eine neue Glashütte, wo er seine Experimente fortsetzte. Er verwendete Metalloxide wie Chrom-, Silber-, Gold-, Kobalt- und sogar Uranoxid in unterschiedlichen Kombinationen, um lichtdurchlässige farbige Gläser zu erreichen. Tiffany behauptete, er habe dreißig Jahre gebraucht, um – gegen die Erwartungen seiner Mitarbeiter – die Ergebnisse zu erreichen, die seinen Vorstellungen entsprachen. 1894 bewilligte das US-Patentamt Tiffany das Warenzeichen »Favrile« für das von ihm entwickelte Glas.

Das Favrile-Glas bedeutete für Tiffany einen wichtigen Durchbruch. Seiner Überzeugung nach übertraf es mit seinen irisierenden Farben qualitativ selbst die besten Gläser, die den Glasmalern der Gotik zur Verfügung gestanden hatten. Er verwendete es für alle seine Buntglasfenster, Lampen, Vasen und Mosaiken. Zwar war irisierendes Glas im 19. Jahrhundert zuvor schon auch von Pantin in Frankreich, Edward Webb in England und Lobmeyer in Österreich produziert worden, doch wirklich populär wurde es erst, als Tiffany und später Loetz in Böhmen ihre Glasobjekte über Bings Pariser Galerie vertreiben ließen. Das Favrile-Glas war Experten zufolge sowohl in gestalterischer – der grenzenlosen Möglichkeiten wegen, atmosphärische Wirkungen zu erreichen – als auch, der immanenten Schönheit des Materials wegen, in dekorativer Hinsicht von emanzipatorischer Bedeutung für die Kunst der Buntglasfenstermosaiken. Das Favrile-Glas wurde seiner Zartheit und seiner magischen Farben wegen bewundert und in der zeitgenössischen Literatur mit »Schmetterlings- und Pfau-

En 1892, Tiffany ouvre sa nouvelle fabrique de verre à Corona, N.Y., où il poursuit constamment ses recherches pour améliorer la qualité de son verre. Il utilise des oxydes métalliques comme le chrome, l'argent, l'or, le cobalt et même l'uranium pour atteindre la transparence requise. Il racontera qu'il lui aura fallu trente ans pour apprendre l'art du verre, en dépit des moqueries de ses collaborateurs qui ne croyaient pas à son procédé. En 1894, l'appelation de verre Favrile, dont il demande l'application à ses verreries, est acceptée.

Pour Tiffany, il s'agit d'une percée de première importance, surpassant, à ses yeux les meilleures verreries du XIIIᵉ siècle. Il va utiliser ce verre Favrile avec ses fascinantes couleurs irisées, pour tous ses vitraux, ses lampes, ses vases et ses mosaïques. Même si le verre irisé avait déjà été fabriqué au XIXᵉ siècle en France par Pantin, en Angleterre par Edward Webb, ou en Autriche par Lobmeyer, ce ne sera que lorsque Tiffany, et plus tard Loetz, en Bohême, commenceront à le commercialiser à grande échelle par l'intermédiaire de la galerie Bing à Paris, que ce verre va connaître son immense succès. Selon certains experts, le verre Favrile est aussi un facteur d'épanouissement pour l'art du vitrail. Il ouvre des possibilités à la fois sur les plans artistique et décoratif : artistique aux possibilités illimitées des effets d'atmosphère, et décoratif en raison de la beauté intrinsèque du matériau. D'ailleurs, le verre Favrile est surtout admiré pour sa délicatesse : dans la littérature de l'époque, on le compare à « des ailes de papillons et de paons, aux couleurs magiques ».

Dans le domaine du verre, Tiffany connaît un adversaire et concurrent redoutable en la personne de John La Farge (1835–1910), qui lui aussi a été peintre et décorateur. Il n'est d'ailleurs pas le seul. Il existe à l'époque à New York plus de soixante-cinq maisons de décoration intérieure et la plupart, d'une manière ou d'une autre, travaillent avec le verre. Tiffany et La Farge vont être les deux designers qui révolutionneront en profondeur le verre teinté, à la fin des années 1870. Avant eux, l'industrie du vitrail avait été de qualité médiocre, sans progrès depuis le Moyen Age. Le verre était peint ou teinté, sans effets de couleurs en provenance du verre lui-même. Tiffany et La Farge parviennent tous deux, par des moyens différents, à une plus grande densité du verre, à une intensité de couleur plus profonde. Il ne fait aucun doute que l'œuvre de

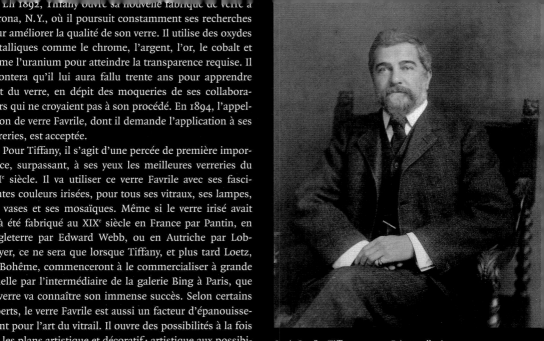

Louis Comfort Tiffany, c. 1915. Private collection.

Detail of a filigree poppy table lamp.
Detail einer filigranen Mohnblumen-Tischlampe.
Détail d'une lampe de table filigrane au motif de coquelicot.
c. 1915. Courtesy Macklowe Gallery, NY.

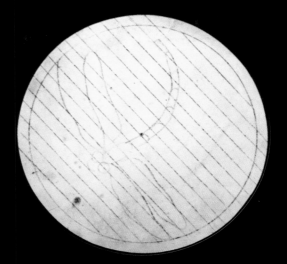

In Amerika hatte Tiffany im Bereich der Glasmalerei einen Gegner und erbitterten Konkurrenten, John La Farge (1835– 1910), der wie er ein Maler und talentierter Künstler war. John La Farge war jedoch nicht der einzige Konkurrent. Damals gab es allein in New York noch 65 weitere Innenausstattungsunternehmen, von denen die meisten auch mit Glas arbeiteten. Sowohl Tiffany als auch La Farge revolutionierten in den späten 70er-Jahren des 19. Jahrhunderts in den Vereinigten Staaten die Kunst der Buntglasfensterherstellung. Sie verwarfen die Technik der Glasbemalung, die sich in den letzten Jahrhunderten durchgesetzt hatte, und griffen stattdessen auf farbige Gläser und damit auf die Technik des Mittelalters zurück, die sie jedoch perfektionierten. Beide erreichten mit ihren jeweiligen Methoden eine größere Dichte und intensivere Farben, und mit Sicherheit übte John La Farge mit seinen Innovationen einen gewissen Einfluss auf Tiffany aus.

Eine weitere Innovation Tiffanys war die Schichtung von mehreren dünnen Glaslagen, wodurch eine größere Farbtiefenwirkung und manchmal sogar ein dreidimensionaler Effekt erreicht werden konnten. Tiffany verfügte ständig über einen Vorrat an Glaslagen in Tausenden verschiedenen Farben, was ihm einen großen Vorteil gegenüber seinen Konkurrenten verschaffte, die sich für gewöhnlich mit den handelsüblichen Glassorten begnügen mussten. Tiffany engagierte die bekanntesten venezianischen und englischen Glasbläser und Chemiker und zahlte ihnen üppige Gehälter, um die von ihm gewünschten Farben und Texturen zu erreichen. Um 1895 produzierte er selbst alle Glas-

La Farge influence Tiffany et le pousse vers certaines innovations techniques.

Tiffany innove aussi avec le verre feuilleté : il superpose une ou plusieurs feuilles de verre pour que les couleurs gagnent en profondeur, parfois avec un effet tridimensionnel. Tiffany a les moyens de puiser dans ses stocks, parmi des milliers de plaques de teintes différentes, ce qui lui confère un avantage certain sur ses concurrents qui ne disposent en général que des plaques en vente dans le commerce. Il engage les souffleurs et les chimistes les plus connus, venus d'Italie ou d'Angleterre, à des salaires très élevés, afin de parvenir aux couleurs et aux textures qu'il souhaite. A partir de 1895, il a créé la gamme de verres dont il a besoin et n'achète plus de verres en plaques. En 1917, dans son discours au Rembrandt Club, il expliquera : « Grâce à des études chimiques et des années d'expérimentation, j'ai trouvé le moyen d'éviter l'utilisation de la peinture, de la gravure, de la chaleur ou de tout autre traitement de la surface du verre. Il est donc désormais possible de fabriquer des personnages en verre, dont la chair même ne doit pas sa couleur à un traitement superficiel, mais à la consistance de ce que j'appellerai le ‹verre naturel› car point n'est besoin d'artifice de verrier pour exprimer la chair. »

En plus de ce handicap technique, La Farge a du mal à trouver autant de clients que Tiffany, mis par sa relation familiale avec la Tiffany & Co. en contact direct et régulier

he last decade of the 19th century. In 1884 Tiffany won a commission to decorate New York's Lyceum Theater by underbidding La Farge. In 1888 he became friendly with the architect Stanford White, who gave him several commissions which La Farge had hoped to garner. In a very short time, the Tiffany Glass Company (later called the Tiffany Glass and Decorating Company) became America's leading supplier of stained glass windows. Among his clients were New York's Colonial Club, James B. Castle, P. B. Griffin and others. Tiffany produced memorial windows depicting several U.S. presidents including Benjamin Harrison, Abraham Lincoln, Theodore Roosevelt, and Chester A. Arthur. Some of the country's most important academic institutions boast Tiffany windows, among them Brown, Columbia, Harvard, Hotchkiss, Princeton and Yale Universities; Dartmouth, Vassar and Wellesley Colleges; and Hotchkiss Academy. Over the course of his career Tiffany received many commissions for stained glass windows from art museums such as the Smithsonian Institution in Washington D. C. and the Chicago Art Institute. He even produced a dramatic window triptych for the Red Cross's headquarters in Washington D. C.

It was through his window designs that Tiffany had first collaborated with S. Bing, and their relationship was to revolutionize the history of decorative art worldwide. Bing's gallery was frequented at the time by the likes of Van Gogh, who browsed Bing's Japanese prints, which later influenced his paintings. Tiffany had visited Bing's gallery when he was in Paris for the 1889 *Exposition Universelle* and was surprised to see that a La Farge window had received much attention and praise. This only served to increase Tiffany's motivation to produce more exciting and better-quality windows. He asked Bing to consider selling his secular windows and other objects in glass, and Bing made a point of visiting Tiffany during a trip to the United States in 1894. Impressed by Tiffany's work, in 1895 Bing commissioned 11 young Parisian artists to create artwork to be translated into Tiffany's glass windows. Among the artists were Pierre Bonnard, Eduard Vuillard and Maurice Denis—all members of the avant-garde art movement known as the *Nabis*—and Henri de Toulouse-Lautrec. Bing's commission put Tiffany at the center of the Parisian and international art scenes, and Tiffany in turn wanted to prove to the world that no

The Russell Sage memorial window in the First Presbyterian Church, one of Tiffany's largest windows.

Das Russel-Sage-Gedächtnisfenster in der Ersten Presbyterianischen Kirche, eines der größten Fenster von Tiffany.

Vitrail commémoratif Russell Sage à l'église First Presbyterian, un des plus grands vitraux de Tiffany.

Far Rockaway, New York, c. 1905. Private collection.

sorten, die er benötigte, und war somit von anderen Glaslieferanten völlig unabhängig. In seiner 1917 im Rembrandt-Club gehaltenen Rede sagte Tiffany: »Mit Hilfe chemischer Studien und durch jahrelange Experimente ist es mir gelungen, ohne die Oberfläche des Glases zu bemalen, zu ätzen, zu brennen oder sonst wie zu behandeln, figürliche Darstellungen in Glas hervorzubringen, bei denen selbst die Fleischtöne nicht durch Oberflächenbehandlung entstanden sind. Die Figuren sind aus, wie ich es nenne, ›genuinem Glas‹ zusammengesetzt, weil es keiner Tricks des Glasmachers bedarf, um Fleischtöne darzustellen.«

Auch in geschäftlicher Hinsicht hatte Tiffany als Sohn des Gründers des weltberühmten Juwelier- und Silbergeschäfts Tiffany & Co. einen unschätzbaren Vorteil gegenüber La Farge. Er hatte gute Verbindungen zu potenziellen Auftraggebern in der gesellschaftlichen Oberschicht und war ein vorzüglicher Geschäftsmann mit großem Marketingtalent, der den wirtschaftlichen Aufschwung in den Vereinigten Staaten in den letzten Jahrzehnten des 19. Jahrhunderts für sich zu nutzen wusste. 1885 konnte er sich gegen La Farge durchsetzen, als der Auftrag für die Innenausstattung des Lyceum Theatre in New York vergeben wurde. Auch der Architekt Stanford White, den er 1888 kennen lernte, gab ihm verschiedene Aufträge, auf die La Farge sich ebenfalls Hoffnungen gemacht hatte. In kürzester Zeit wurde die Tiffany Glass Company (später Tiffany Glass & Decorating Company) zum wichtigsten Lieferanten für Buntglasfenster in Amerika. Zu ihren Auftraggebern zählten unter anderen der New Yorker Colonial Club, James B. Castle und P. B. Griffin. Tiffany schuf Memorial-Fenster mit Darstellungen verschiedener Präsidenten wie Benjamin Harrison, Abraham Lincoln, Theodore Roosevelt und Chester A. Arthur. Er fertigte Fenster für einige der wichtigsten akademischen Institutionen der USA, zum Beispiel für die Universitäten Yale, Princeton, Harvard, Columbia, Brown und Hotchkiss, für die Colleges Vassar, Dartmouth und Wellesley sowie für Kunstmuseen wie das Smithsonian in Washington, D. C., und das Art Institute in Chicago. Für die Zentrale des amerikanischen Roten Kreuzes stellte er ein dramatisches dreiteiliges Fenster her.

Über seine Glasfensterentwürfe kam Tiffany auch mit Siegfried Bing in Kontakt, und aus dieser ersten Begegnung ging eine Verbindung hervor, die die Geschichte der dekorativen Kunst revolutionieren sollte. Bings Galerie

avec ceux en position de passer commande. Tiffany sait utiliser son extraordinaire compétence commerciale, son sens aigu des affaires et ses liens avec le monde des nantis pour profiter de l'opulence économique dans laquelle baignent les Etats-Unis dans les dix dernières années du XIXᵉ siècle. En 1884, il obtient commande pour la décoration du Lyceum Theatre à New York en proposant un prix moins élevé que La Farge. En 1888, il se lie d'amitié avec l'architecte Stanford White, qui lui confie plusieurs commandes que La Farge avait espéré remporter. Très vite, la Tiffany Glass Co. (qui allait prendre le nom de Tiffany Glass and Decorating Co.) devient le premier fournisseur de vitraux américain. Parmi ses clients, on compte le Colonial Club de New York, James B. Castle, P. B. Griffin et bien d'autres. Tiffany fournit des vitraux commémoratifs, représentant divers présidents américains dont Benjamin Harrison, Abraham Lincoln, Theodore Roosevelt et Chester A. Arthur. Certaines institutions universitaires, parmi les plus réputées, s'enorgueillissent de vitraux Tiffany, en particulier Yale, Princeton, Dartmouth College, Harvard, Columbia, Brown, Vassar College, Wellesley College et Hotchkiss University. Au cours de sa longue carrière, Tiffany reçoit de nombreuses commandes de vitraux pour des musées comme la Smithsonian Institution à Washington D. C. ou le Chicago Art Institute. Il fabrique même un impressionnant triptyque pour le siège social de la Croix Rouge à Washington D. C.

Ayant commencé sa collaboration avec S. Bing grâce à ses vitraux, Tiffany va ensuite, avec ce dernier, révolutionner l'histoire des arts décoratifs, dans le monde entier. À l'époque, la galerie Bing est surtout fréquentée par des gens comme Van Gogh, qui venait là admirer les estampes japonaises et s'en inspirer pour ses peintures. Tiffany visite pour la première fois la galerie Bing lors de son voyage pour l'Exposition Universelle de 1889 et découvre, à sa grande surprise, l'accueil très favorable réservé alors à un vitrail de La Farge. Cela ne fait que renforcer sa motivation à produire des vitraux encore plus beaux et plus remarquables. Il demande alors à Bing s'il accepterait de se charger de la vente de ses vitraux et autres objets en verre. Quand il vient aux Etats-Unis, en 1894, Bing va donc rendre visite à Tiffany. Impressionné par ce qu'il découvre, Bing commande en 1895, à onze jeunes artistes parisiens des projets qui ont été transposés en verre sur vitraux Tif-

painting could capture the brilliance of light and color as beautifully as his windows did. Shortly after Tiffany's Four Seasons window series had been exhibited in Paris in the *Exposition Universelle* of 1900, Bing displayed them at the Grafton Galleries in London. From all accounts they won praise for the vibrant colors of their compositions depicting the seasons of the year in colorful landscapes, florals and spectacular renderings of nature. Bing and Tiffany remained friends and business associates until Bing's death in 1905.

Churches, synagogues and other houses of worship seemed to spring up overnight in this period of economic prosperity. In 1875 more than 4,000 new churches of various denominations were under construction. For earlier cathedrals and smaller houses of worship, stained glass windows that were often of inferior quality had been imported from England and other European countries, but Tiffany and his wealthy clients helped improve this situation. The first of his many ecclesiastical window commissions was for St. Mark's Episcopal Church in Islip, New York, in 1878. In the mid-1880's Tiffany instituted an ecclesiastical department to help decorate the thousands of newly built churches and synagogues, printing brochures offering stained glass windows, mosaics, frescoes, and altars as well as portable objects such as crucifixes, lamps, lecterns, sacred vessels, needlework, statues and more. The subjects of the figurative windows in churches, synagogues, mausoleums and commemorative chapels were based on Biblical themes and the lives of saints, sometimes using motifs from traditional paintings by artists such as Botticelli, Raphael, and Tiffany's English contemporary, William Holman Hunt (1827–1910). Later ecclesiastical windows included depictions of landscapes to which Tiffany attributed religious significance.

Tiffany's most ambitious ecclesiastical project by far was a spectacular Byzantine-style chapel interior designed, at S. Bing's suggestion, for the 1893 World's Columbian Exposition in Chicago. Located in his father's corporate pavilion, the chapel drew over a million visitors and great international acclaim, and Tiffany was awarded no fewer than 54 medals for his varied exhibit at the exposition. According to Bing, Tiffany had "discovered how to adapt the lofty character of Byzantine splendor to contemporary taste." The interior of the chapel consisted of irid-

wurde damals auch von Avantgardekünstlern wie van Gogh besucht, der sich dort von japanischen Graphiken inspirieren ließ. 1889 reiste Tiffany zur Weltausstellung nach Paris, wo zu seiner Überraschung ein Buntglasfenster seines Konkurrenten John La Farge große Beachtung und Zustimmung fand. Für Tiffany war das ein Ansporn, die Qualität seiner eigenen Fenster noch zu steigern. Er suchte Bing in seiner Galerie auf und machte ihm den Vorschlag, seine säkularen Glasfenster und andere Glasobjekte in das Programm der Galerie aufzunehmen. Als Bing 1894 in die Vereinigten Staaten reiste, besuchte er Tiffany in New York und war von seinen Arbeiten tief beeindruckt. 1895 gab er bei elf jungen französischen Künstlern – darunter Pierre Bonnard, Edouard Vuillard und Maurice Denis, allesamt Mitglieder der als »Nabis« bekannten Avantgardebewegung sowie Henri de Toulouse-Lautrec – Glasfenstervorlagen für Tiffany in Auftrag. Bings Auftrag rückte Tiffany in den Mittelpunkt der Pariser und der internationalen Kunstszene und gab ihm die Möglichkeit, der Welt zu beweisen, dass die Brillanz des Lichts und der Farben seiner Glasfenster von keinem Gemälde übertroffen werden konnte. Tiffanys Buntglasfenster *The Four Seasons* (»Die vier Jahreszeiten«) wurde auf der Pariser Weltausstellung von 1900 präsentiert, und Bing ließ es kurz darauf auch in den Grafton Galleries in London ausstellen. Die glühenden Farben und die Komposition mit ihren farbenfrohen Landschaften, Blumen und spektakulären Naturszenen brachten dem Fenster große Bewunderung ein. Bis zu Bings Tod im Jahre 1905 blieben er und Tiffany Freunde und Geschäftspartner.

Kirchen und andere Gotteshäuser schienen in den USA in dieser prosperierenden Zeit regelrecht aus dem Boden zu schießen. Im Jahre 1875 waren mehr als 4000 neue Kirchen verschiedenster Glaubensgemeinschaften im Bau. Die Buntglasfenster für die frühen Kathedralen und kleineren Gotteshäuser waren aus England und anderen europäischen Ländern importiert worden und oft von minderer Qualität. Tiffany und seine wohlhabenden Auftraggeber trugen zur Verbesserung dieser Situation bei. Sein erstes von vielen Kirchenfenstern schuf er 1878 für die St. Mark's Episcopal Church in Islip auf Long Island. Um 1885 richtete Tiffany eine spezielle sakrale Abteilung ein, um neu errichtete Kirchen und Synagogen mit Buntglasfenstern, Mosaiken, Fresken und Altären sowie tragbaren Objekten wie Kruzifixen, Lampen, Chorpulten, sakralen Gefäßen und

any. Parmi eux, figurent Pierre Bonnard, Édouard Vuillard et Maurice Denis – tous trois membres du mouvement avant-gardiste des Nabis. Cette commande de Bing place Tiffany au centre de la scène artistique parisienne et internationale, et il est bien déterminé à prouver au monde qu'aucune peinture ne saurait saisir l'éclat de la lumière et de la couleur mieux que ses vitraux. Quand son panneau, « Les Quatre saisons » est présenté à l'Exposition Universelle de 1900, Bing décide de l'exposer aux Grafton Galleries de Londres, immédiatement après. Selon tous les témoignages, l'œuvre est acclamée pour ses couleurs éclatantes et sa composition sur le thème des saisons, avec des paysages colorés, des motifs floraux, et d'impressionnants rendus de la nature. Bing et Tiffany devaient rester amis et associés jusqu'à la mort de Bing, en 1905.

En cette période de prospérité économique, il semble qu'églises et autres lieux de culte surgissent de partout. En 1875, plus de quatre mille églises, de toutes dénominations, sont en construction. Pour les cathédrales et les édifices moins importants, les vitraux, souvent de qualité médiocre, étaient jusque là, importés d'Angleterre ou d'autres pays européens. Grâce à Tiffany et à ses riches clients, la situation va changer. En 1878, la première de ses nombreuses commandes religieuses est destinée à l'église épiscopale St. Mark de Islip à New York. Vers 1885, Tiffany crée un département ecclésiastique, destiné à assurer la décoration des milliers d'églises et de synagogues récemment construites, et publie des brochures proposant vitraux, mosaïques, fresques, autels ou autres objets transportables tels que crucifix, lampes, lutrins, patènes, broderies, statues, etc. Dans les églises, les synagogues, les mausolées et les chapelles commémoratives, les sujets des vitraux sont puisés dans la Bible et la vie des saints, s'inspirant parfois de peintures traditionnelles dues à des artistes comme Botticelli, Raphaël ou le contemporain britannique de Tiffany, William Holman Hunt (1827–1910). Par la suite, sur ces panneaux religieux, on verra apparaître des paysages auxquels Tiffany attribue une signification religieuse.

Son projet de loin le plus ambitieux sera un intérieur de chapelle d'inspiration néo-byzantine, conçu sur la suggestion de Bing, à l'occasion de l'Exposition Colombienne Internationale de Chicago, en 1893. Installée dans le pavillon de l'entreprise de son père, la chapelle attire plus d'un

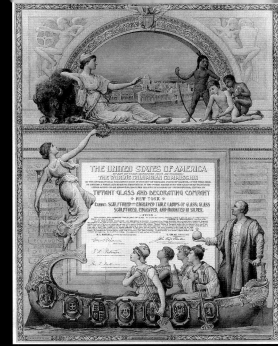

Certificate of merit awarded for Tiffany's lavish display at the 1893 Exposition, including a Byzantine chapel and two additional showrooms.

Ehrenurkunde für Tiffanys großzügigen Beitrag zur Weltausstellung von 1893, wozu eine Byzantinische Kapelle und zwei zusätzliche Ausstellungsräume gehörten

Certificat de mérite adressé à Tiffany pour sa somptueuse présentation a l'Exposition Colombienne Internationale de 1893 qui comportait une chapelle byzantine et deux autres salles d'exposition

Courtesy Alastair Duncan, NY.

scent glass objects, glass mosaics, marble products and 12 glass windows presenting the entire ecclesiastical range of his company. Huge classical columns and arches were built for the 800-square-foot interior. The effect created by light filtering through the intense colors of the stained glass windows was, by all accounts, nothing less than spectacular.

On October 30, 1893, the last day of the Chicago Exhibition, Mrs. Celia Whipple Wallace (known as Chicago's "Diamond Queen") purchased the chapel for $50,000 and donated it to the Episcopal Cathedral of St. John the Divine in New York, which was still under construction at that time. The chapel remained there for about ten years. Unchecked water damage took its toll on the architecture and decoration of the chapel, and it was sealed off in 1911. In 1916 Tiffany removed it at his own expense. After substantial repairs he had the chapel installed at Laurelton Hall, his luxurious Long Island estate. In 1946 parts of it were auctioned off, and after Laurelton Hall was ravaged by fire in 1957, most of the chapel was saved by Jeannette McKean, Tiffany's granddaughter, and her husband Hugh F. McKean. The McKeans later established a gallery in Winter Park, Florida, The Charles Hosmer Morse Museum of American Art, and purchased additional Tiffany works to fill it. It now contains one of the most extensive collections of Tiffany's creations in the world. Until 1997, most of the chapel's elements remained in crates while the McKeans searched for the dispersed items. They succeed-

A five-part magnolia and wisteria window Tiffany designed for this bay in his luxurious Manhattan home.

Fünfteilige Bleiverglasung mit Magnolien- und Wistariendekor, von Tiffany für diese Nische in seinem luxuriösen Haus in Manhattan entworfen.

Vitraux en cinq parties avec des motifs de magnolias et de glycines conçus par Tiffany pour sa luxueuse maison à Manhattan.

c. 1885. Private collection.

Fenster für Kirchen, Synagogen, Mausoleen und Gedächtniskapellen zeigen oft biblische Sujets und Heiligendarstellungen, die manchmal populären Gemälden von Botticelli, Raffael und Tiffanys englischem Zeitgenossen William Holman Hunt (1827–1910) entnommen waren. Die späteren sakralen Fenster zeigen Landschaftsdarstellungen, die Tiffany mit religiösen Konnotationen auflud.

Tiffanys ehrgeizigstes sakrales Projekt war eine spektakuläre Kapelle im byzantinischen Stil, die er auf S. Bings Anregung hin für die Chicagoer Weltausstellung von 1893 entwarf. Die Kapelle wurde im Pavillon der Firma seines Vaters eingerichtet, zog über 1 Mio. Besucher an und brachte Tiffany 54 Medaillen und internationale Anerkennung ein. Wie Bing sagte, war es Tiffany gelungen, »die erhabene byzantinische Pracht dem zeitgenössischen Geschmack anzupassen«. Die Ausstattung dieser Kapelle, in der die sakrale Produktpalette seines Unternehmens präsentiert wurde, bestand aus Objekten aus irisierendem Glas, Glasmosaiken, Marmorgegenständen und zwölf Buntglasfenstern. Für den 74 m² großen Innenraum wurden riesige klassische Säulen und Bögen errichtet. Das Licht, das durch die Buntglasfenster mit ihren intensiven Farben gefiltert wurde, bot den Besuchern ein faszinierendes Schauspiel.

Am 30. Oktober 1893, dem letzten Tag der Weltausstellung, erwarb die als »Diamantenkönigin« von Chicago bekannte Celia Whipple Wallace die Kapelle für 50 000 Dollar und stiftete sie der damals noch im Bau befindlichen Episkopalkathedrale St. John the Divine in New York, wo sie ungefähr zehn Jahre lang stand. 1911 wurde die Kapelle aufgrund eines Wasserschadens versiegelt, und 1916 ließ Tiffany sie auf seine Kosten aus der Kathedrale entfernen und nach beträchtlichen Instandsetzungsarbeiten auf dem Gelände seines Landsitzes Laurelton Hall auf Long Island aufstellen. 1946 wurden Teile der Kapelle versteigert. Als 1957 ein Brand auf Tiffanys Anwesen wütete, konnte der größte Teil der Kapelle von Hugh F. McKean und seiner Frau Jeanette, Tiffanys Enkelin, gerettet werden. McKean gehörte zu den jungen Künstlern, die von der Tiffany Foundation gefördert wurden und in Laurelton Hall wohnen durften. Später gründeten die McKeans ein Museum in Winter Park in Florida, The Charles Hosmer Morse Museum of American Art, und erwarben weitere Werke Tiffanys. Heute besitzt das Museum eine der weltweit bestsortierten Tiffany-Sammlun-

ainsi qu'une large reconnaissance internationale. Selon Bing, Tiffany a « découvert le moyen d'adapter la noblesse et la splendeur byzantine au goût contemporain ». L'intérieur de la chapelle comprend des objets en verre irisé, des mosaïques de verre, des œuvres en marbre, ainsi que douze vitraux offrant un panorama complet de l'offre de sa fabrique en matière ecclésiastique. D'énormes arcades et colonnes classiques sont construites pour un intérieur de 80 m². La lumière filtrant à travers les vitraux aux couleurs profondes est, s'accorde-t-on à dire, tout simplement splendide.

Le 30 octobre 1893, dernier jour de l'Exposition de Chicago, Mrs Celia Whipple Wallace (surnommée « La Reine du Diamant ») fait l'acquisition de la chapelle pour 50 000 dollars et l'offre à la cathédrale épiscopale de St. John the Divine de New York, alors encore en construction. La chapelle y restera environ dix ans. D'importants dégâts causés par les eaux vont endommager son architecture et sa décoration et, en 1911, l'accès au public sera interdit. En 1916 Tiffany la fait démonter à ses frais. Après d'importantes réparations, il la fait réinstaller à Laurelton Hall, sa luxueuse propriété de Long Island. En 1946, certaines parties sont vendues aux enchères puis, après un incendie dévastateur en 1957, la plus grande partie de la chapelle est sauvée par Hugh F. McKean et sa femme Jeannette, petite-fille de Tiffany. Plus tard, le couple Kean ouvre un musée à Winter Park, en Floride, Le Charles Hosmer Morse Museum, et achète d'autres œuvres de Tiffany pour l'enrichir. Il contient aujourd'hui l'une des plus belles collections d'œuvres de Tiffany au monde. Jusqu'en 1997, la plupart des éléments de la chapelle restent en caisses, tandis que le couple McKean recherche les éléments dispersés. Ils parviennent à les retrouver et, en 1997 le conseil d'administration du Morse Museum vote la reconstruction et la restauration de l'édifice. Une équipe d'architectes, d'artistes et d'experts en conservation travaille sur le projet pendant plus de deux ans. La chapelle est enfin inaugurée pour le public en avril 1999, pour la première fois depuis 1911.

Outre les commandes religieuses, les ateliers de Tiffany produisent des vitraux mythologiques et historiques ainsi que ces paysages qu'il affectionne particulièrement et où abondent les fleurs. Bon nombre de panneaux sont extrêmement ornementaux, avec incrustations de médaillons. Il réalise aussi quelques vitraux abstraits dans les

ed in locating the missing furnishings, and in 1997 the Morse Museum's board voted to reassemble and restore the chapel. A team of architects, artists and conservation experts worked on the project for more than two years, and the chapel was finally opened to the public, for the first time since 1911, in April 1999.

In addition to ecclesiastical commissions, Tiffany's studios produced mythological and historical windows, as well as a wide variety of his beloved landscapes, abundant with flowers, plants and trees. Many of his windows were ornate with inset medallions. He also produced a few abstract windows, in which nature was still pervasive. Even Tiffany's critics acknowledged and admired his mastery of glass technique, his inventiveness, and above all his undeniable mastery as a colorist. Some critics derided his designs as "kitsch" and his colors as being too bright, almost gaudy. Tiffany's reply to accusations of commercialism was that he worked and designed his windows for the industrial age. Because of the great demand for his windows, he felt he had to expand into manufacturing on an industrial scale. Despite the large scale, however, he personally supervised every stage of production, from the first sketches of a design to the selection of the glass and the actual manufacturing.

According to Hugh McKean, late fellow of the Tiffany Foundation, "Tiffany's role in making the windows varied according to circumstances. All began with a sketch, possibly by Tiffany but most often by a staff artist." In a series of steps, the final approved sketch was duplicated on paper, or architect's linen, from which templates for the individual pattern pieces were created for the glasscutters. McKean describes the expertise required by the glasscutters: "Careful consideration had to be given to the type of glass needed in each part of the design and to the shape and size of each piece. Another factor to consider was the limitations of the glass. Some cuts are relatively easy and some are impossible. Some kinds of glass, notably drapery glass, are difficult to cut. It was also important to Tiffany that the design of the pieces of glass had 'rhythm and flow'."

Quality was of such critical importance to Tiffany that he insisted on employing the services of the very best craftsmen, such as the Venetian glassblower Andrea Boldini and the English artisan Arthur Nash.

Sketch for a stained glass window by a Tiffany employee, with Tiffany's signature of approval (not visible).

Entwurfszeichnung eines Mitarbeiters von Tiffany für eine Bleiverglasung, von Tiffany per Signatur bewilligt (nicht sichtbar).

Ebauche pour un vitrail réalisée par un collègue de Tiffany, que ce dernier approuva par sa signature (non visible).

Courtesy Phillips Auctioneers, NY.

n Kisten aufbewahrt; die McKeans hatten bis dahin nach den fehlenden Teilen gesucht, die 1946 versteigert worden waren. Tatsächlich gelang es ihnen, die fehlenden Teile und Ausstattungsgegenstände aufzuspüren, und 1997 fasste das Direktorium des Morse Museums den Beschluss, die Kapelle zu restaurieren und wieder aufzubauen. Mehr als zwei Jahre lang waren ein Team von Architekten sowie mehrere Kunst- und Restaurierungsexperten mit diesem Projekt beschäftigt. Im April 1999 wurde sie – erstmals seit 1911 – der Öffentlichkeit zugänglich gemacht.

Neben sakralen Auftragsarbeiten entstanden in den Tiffany-Studios auch Fenster mit mythologischen und historischen Themen, Landschaften voller Blumen sowie einige abstrakte Fenster, in denen jedoch die Natur immer eine Rolle spielte. Dabei waren viele Fenster extrem ornamental gehalten mit eingesetzten Medaillons. Einige Kritiker schmähten Tiffanys Entwürfe als kitschig und seine Farben als zu leuchtend und grell. Jedoch bewunderten selbst diese seine technische Meisterschaft und Erfindungsgabe. Sein Rang als außerordentlicher Kolorist war unbestritten. Dem Vorwurf der Kommerzialisierung seiner Kunst hielt Tiffany entgegen, dass er Fenster für das Industriezeitalter entwerfe und produziere. Der großen Nachfrage wegen hatte seine Glasfensterproduktion industrielle Ausmaße angenommen. Trotz der umfangreichen Auftragslage überwachte Tiffany persönlich jeden einzelnen Herstellungsschritt: von den ersten Skizzen über die Auswahl des Glases bis zur eigentlichen Fertigung.

Hugh McKean zufolge war »Tiffanys eigener Anteil am Entstehungsprozess von Fall zu Fall verschieden. Am Anfang stand immer eine Skizze, manchmal von Tiffanys eigener Hand, meistens jedoch von einem künstlerischen Mitarbeiter.« In einer Folge von Arbeitsschritten wurde dann der endgültige Entwurf auf Papier oder Leinenpergament übertragen, woraus dann Schablonen geschnitten wurden, die den Glasschneidern als Vorlagen dienten. Die Ausführung übernahmen erfahrene Fachleute: »Große Sorgfalt war bei der Auswahl des Glases für die einzelnen Teile des Entwurfs und bei der Festlegung der Form und Größe der einzelnen Stücke vonnöten. Außerdem waren die spezifischen Probleme bei der Verarbeitung der unterschiedlichen Glassorten zu bedenken. Einige Schnitte sind relativ problemlos, andere dagegen nicht durchführbar.

admirent chez Tiffany sa maîtrise de la technique du verre, son inventivité et par-dessus tout, ses talents incontestables de coloriste. Certains qualifient ses dessins de « kitsch » et trouvent ses couleurs trop brillantes, presque criardes. Aux accusations de mercantilisme, il répond qu'il travaille et conçoit ses vitraux pour l'ère industrielle. Etant donné la forte demande pour ses vitraux, il doit produire désormais à une échelle industrielle. Malgré la quantité, c'est lui, en personne, qui chaque jour supervise la production, de l'élaboration des esquisses à la sélection du verre et la fabrication finale.

Selon Hugh McKean, ancien membre de la Tiffany Foundation, « dans la fabrication des vitraux, le rôle de Tiffany variait selon les circonstances. Tout commençait par une esquisse, parfois de la main de Tiffany, mais plus souvent par un des artistes de l'équipe. » En une série d'étapes, l'esquisse finalement retenue était reproduite sur toile d'architecte, à partir de quoi un patron pour chaque élément était fabriqué à l'intention des coupeurs de verre. McKean décrit le parfait savoir-faire exigé de ces derniers :

« Il faut accorder la plus grande attention au type de verre nécessaire à chacune des parties, à la forme et à la taille de chaque pièce. Il faut aussi prendre en compte un autre facteur : les limites du verre. Certaines coupes sont relativement faciles, d'autres impossibles. Certaines sortes de verre, notamment le verre drapé, sont difficiles à couper. Pour Tiffany, il était aussi essentiel que le dessin des divers éléments possède ‹rythme et fluidité›. »

La qualité est d'une importance si cruciale aux yeux de Tiffany, qu'il insiste toujours pour engager les meilleurs artisans, comme le souffleur vénitien Andrea Boldini ou l'Anglais Arthur Nash.

Le nom de Louis Comfort Tiffany restera dans toutes les mémoires pour la beauté de son verre Favrile et pour ces vitraux qu'il produit par milliers. Selon Alastair Duncan, un expert de Tiffany, les vitraux, à l'origine, varient entre 3500 et 5000 dollars, ce qui à l'époque, est considéré comme cher. On les trouve partout, aux Etats-Unis, en Europe, en Amérique du Sud, en Australie et même au Japon, où un musée entier est consacré à Tiffany. Se trouver en présence d'un de ses vitraux, est toujours, sur le plan esthétique, une expérience émouvante.

bered for the beauty of his Favrile glass and his stained glass windows, of which approximately 5,000 were produced. According to Tiffany expert Alastair Duncan, prices for Tiffany's windows originally ranged from $3,500 to $5,000, and were considered expensive at the time. They can be found all over the United States, Europe, Latin America, Australia and even Japan, where an entire museum is dedicated to his work. To be in the presence of a Tiffany stained glass window is always a moving aesthetic experience. Tiffany's window production flourished between 1900 and 1910, but quickly declined even before the advent of World War I. In 1920 Tiffany was already 72 years old, and the quality of the windows manufactured by his company deteriorated markedly with his retirement several years later.

Tiffany's lamps and shades: Color upon light

The sovereign importance of color is only beginning to be realized. (Louis Comfort Tiffany)

Though the lamp can be traced back in history nearly as far as the discovery of fire, Thomas Edison's introduction of the electric bulb was a sensation and revolutionized the variety and placement of light sources in the home. The advent of the electrical era coincided with the emergence of Art Nouveau and Tiffany, ever open to a new opportunity in both business and aesthetics, leaped to the challenge of using electric light to coax new beauty from his extraordinary colors. He softened electricity's harsh light with the beautiful glass lampshades that were to become key icons of Art Nouveau worldwide. Coincidentally, in 1885 Edison and Tiffany both decorated James Steel MacKaye's spectacular Lyceum Theater in New York; later, in the 1920's, they maintained social contact because they each had a retirement home in adjoining Florida towns.

To many people throughout the world, the name Tiffany brings to mind his stunning lampshades. Artistically, however, his stained glass windows preceded them; production of his more popular lampshades was a by-product using the many thousands of pieces of glass that remained after cutting individual elements for the windows. Tiffany began selling blown-glass shades in the mid-

zu schneiden. Darüber hinaus legte Tiffany bei der Gestaltung der Glasstücke großen Wert auf ›Rhythmus und Fluss‹.«

Qualität war für Tiffany von überragender Bedeutung, und er beschäftigte die besten Fachkräfte seiner Zeit wie etwa den venezianischen Glasbläser Andrea Boldini und den englischen Kunsthandwerker Arthur Nash.

Dem Tiffany-Experten Alastair Duncan zufolge kosteten Tiffanys Fenster zwischen 3500 und 5000 Dollar und waren damit für ihre Zeit sehr teuer. Denoch finden sie sich in allen Teilen der USA, in Europa, Lateinamerika, Australien und sogar in Japan, wo seinem Werk ein ganzes Museum gewidmet ist.

Die Blütezeit seiner Buntglasfensterproduktion lag zwischen 1900 und 1910, doch bereits vor dem Ausbruch des Ersten Weltkriegs ging die Produktion schnell zurück. 1920 war Tiffany bereits 72 Jahre alt, und als er sich einige Jahre später ins Privatleben zurückzog, setzte ein merklicher Rückgang der Qualität der in seinen Werkstätten gefertigten Glasfenster ein.

Farbe auf Licht: Tiffanys Lampen und Lampenschirme

Wir sind eben erst dabei, die herausragende Bedeutung der Farbe zu erfassen. (L. C. T.)

Die Geschichte der Lampe lässt sich fast bis zur Entdeckung des Feuers zurückverfolgen. Schon in der frühen Menschheitsgeschichte wurden Öllampen aus Ton, Stein und Muscheln gefertigt, und die Ägypter, Griechen und Römer sind für ihre dekorativ gestalteten Lampen bekannt. Die elektrische Glühbirne, die 1879 von Thomas Alva Edison der Öffentlichkeit vorgestellt wurde, war eine Sensation und revolutionierte die Einsatzmöglichkeiten der künstlichen Beleuchtung. Der Beginn des Zeitalters der Elektrizität fiel mit der Blütezeit des Jugendstils zusammen, der internationalen Kunstbewegung, die in Amerika von Tiffany repräsentiert wurde. Tiffany stand zeit seines Lebens

Entre 1900 et 1910, la production des vitraux prospère
mais juste avant la Première Guerre mondiale, elle com
mence à décliner rapidement. En 1920, Tiffany est âgé d
72 ans. La qualité des vitraux fabriqués dans ses ateliers s
détériorera et ce de manière notable, quand il prendra s
retraite, quelques années plus tard.

Couleur sur lumière : lampes et abat-jour Tiffany

*L'importance absolue de la couleur commence seulement à êtr
reconnue. (Louis Comfort Tiffany)*

Si la lampe apparaît dans l'histoire presque dès la décou
verte du feu, l'introduction de l'ampoule à incandescence
par Thomas Edison, fait sensation et révolutionne la qualit
et la localisation des sources de lumière à l'intérieur de l
maison. L'arrivée de la fée électricité coïncide avec l'émer
gence de l'Art Nouveau, mouvement international don
Tiffany est, en Amérique, le principal représentant. Tou
jours ouvert à toute nouveauté commerciale ou esthétique
Tiffany relève le défi de l'électricité qui va conférer un
beauté nouvelle à ses couleurs extraordinaires. Il adouci
la lumière crue de l'électricité au moyen de magnifique
abat-jour de verre qui allaient devenir le symbole de l'Ar
Nouveau. Par hasard, il se trouve qu'en 1885, Edison e
Tiffany sont tous deux choisis pour décorer le magnifiqu
Lyceum Theater de New York, propriété de James Stee
MacKaye. Plus tard, dans les années 1920, Tiffany et Edi
son continueront de se fréquenter, car ils se retrouveron
en Floride, où tous deux se sont retirés.

Pour beaucoup de gens, et dans le monde entier, l
nom de Tiffany évoque ces fantastiques lampes de verre
On ne sait pas toujours que, du point de vue artistique, se
vitraux furent créés en premier. La fabrication de ses abat
jour les plus célèbres a d'abord constitué une production
secondaire, pour utiliser les milliers de morceaux de verr
restant après la coupe des éléments destinés aux vitraux
Tiffany commença à vendre des abat-jour en verre souffl
vers 1895, et ceux en mosaïque de verre aux alentours d
1898. La production culmine entre 1900 et 1914, même s
elle se poursuit jusqu'à la fin des années 1930. Ce
lampes vont permettre à plus de gens d'apprécier l
beauté saisissante du verre Favrile, et d'en acheter pou
leur foyer. À l'origine, l'inspiration de ces lampes étai

Working drawing for a daffodil and narcissus lampshade.

Entwurfszeichnung für einen Lampenschirm mit Osterglocken-
und Narzissendekor.

*Ebauche d'un abat-jour en filigrane avec des motifs de jonquilles
et de narcisses.*

38.7 x 51.4 cm. Christie's Images.

Pictures from a brochure featuring the exterior and an interior view of lamp production at the Corona glass factory.

Fotografien aus einer Broschüre, die eine Außen- und eine Innenansicht der Corona-Glasfabrik zeigen.

Photos d'une brochure de la fabrique à Corona représentant l'extérieur et l'intérieur de la production de lampes.

C. 1914. Private collection.

Lampshade production at Tiffany Glass & Decorating Co.

Lampenschirmproduktion in der Tiffany Glass & Decorating Co.

Production d'abat-jour à la Tiffany Glass & Decorating Co.

1898. Courtesy Alastair Duncan, NY.

1890's and leaded glass shades around 1898. Peak production of Tiffany lamps occurred between 1900 and 1914 although they continued to be made well into the 1930's. The lamps allowed more people to appreciate the striking beauty of Favrile glass and to enjoy it in their very homes. The subjects of his lamps were primarily floral, with seemingly limitless range of colors; however, Tiffany also designed lamps with geometric patterns. The lamp base was usually made of metal (in some cases with mosaic sometimes designed for a particular shade pattern but most often able to be combined with any shade. No one knows precisely how many lamps were produced in total but a 1906 catalogue listed over 300 available models.

In 1900 an average Tiffany lamp was priced at $100 with smaller lamps starting at $40. They were luxury items that no well-to-do American who wished to live in style was willing to do without. Wealthy Europeans were able to acquire them in Paris from S. Bing's gallery, Tiffany's exclusive European representative. Nevertheless, although most of his private clients were America's wealthiest families and his works were high-priced for their time, he felt that spending large amounts of money was not necessarily a prerequisite for creating a beautiful home. He said in 1910: "Extravagance does not produce beauty; and many of our richest people, like some of our poor people, have not yet come to see the value of good taste. In fact, money is frequently an absolute bar to good taste, for it leads to show and over-elaboration."

en offen gegenüber und griff die Herausforderung auf, mit Hilfe des elektrischen Lichts die außergewöhnlichen Farben seines Favrile-Glases in neuem Glanz erstrahlen zu lassen. Mit seinen herrlichen bleiverglasten Lampenschirmen, die zum Inbegriff des Jugendstils wurden, wusste Tiffany das gleißende elektrische Licht effektvoll zu dämpfen. 1885 ergab es sich, dass Edison und Tiffany im Auftrag von James Steel MacKaye gemeinsam an der Innenausstattung des Lyceum Theatre in New York arbeiten konnten, und als sie später, in den 20er-Jahren, sich beide in Florida zur Ruhe setzten, pflegten sie weiterhin den Kontakt.

Viele Menschen in aller Welt denken bei dem Namen Tiffany zunächst an seine atemberaubend schönen Lampen. Ursprünglich waren die Lampenschirme allerdings nur »Nebenprodukte« aus den Tausenden kleinerer Glasfragmente, die bei der Produktion der bleiverglasten Fenster übrig blieben. Die ersten Lampenschirme aus geblasenem Glas entstanden um 1895, die ersten bleiverglasten um 1898. Die Produktion hatte ihre Blütezeit zwischen 1900 und 1914 und wurde bis weit in die 30er-Jahre hinein fortgesetzt. Die Lampen boten einer breiteren Bevölkerungsschicht die Möglichkeit, sich in der privaten

paremment sans limite. Toutefois, Tiffany crée aussi des lampes à motifs géométriques. Le pied est généralement en métal, parfois conçu pour un abat-jour en particulier mais le plus souvent adaptable à tout modèle. Nul ne sai précisément le nombre total de lampes qui est produi alors. Mais un catalogue daté de 1906 présente une liste comprenant pas moins de 300 modèles disponibles.

En 1900, une lampe standard est cotée en moyenne à environ 100 dollars et à 40 pour les plus petites. Il s'agi d'articles de luxe dont aucun Américain aisé, désirant vivre dans un certain raffinement, ne saurait se passer. Les Européens riches peuvent les acquérir à Paris, à la Galerie Bing représentant exclusif de Tiffany. Pourtant, même si la plupart de ses clients privés sont de riches Américains e si ses objets sont chers pour l'époque, Tiffany sait que dépenser de grosses sommes d'argent ne suffit pas pou créer un bel intérieur. En 1910, il explique : « Ce n'est pa la dépense excessive qui engendre la beauté, et nombre de no citoyens les plus riches, comme d'autres plus pauvres n'ont pas encore compris la valeur du bon goût. En fait l'argent est souvent un obstacle au bon goût, car il mène à l'étalage et à trop de complications. »

Tiffany's lamps merged in.) had models, from simple to complex, small to large, from quite plain to sumptuous and elaborate. There were lamps shaped like cones and globes, table lamps, floor lamps and hanging lamps (some models of which Tiffany dubbed "hanging bouquets"). However, it is the floral lamps, with their characteristic ornate bronze bases, some of which incorporate glass mosaics, that are most highly sought by collectors today. The wide variety of flowers Tiffany used as subjects for his shades includes geraniums, magnolias, poppies, clematis, poinsettia, water lilies, daffodils, tulips, peonies, nasturtiums, narcissi, begonias, hydrangeas, laburnum, roses, apple and cherry blossoms, and wisteria. He also used bamboo leaves and grapevines as well as exotic fruit such as pineapple. Certain shade styles—such as the Elizabethan, Empire Jewel, Venetian, and Russian models—recall periods in history. His Dragonfly shade was extremely popular, and was produced in a wide variety of shapes, sizes and colors. Some of the complex designs incorporate over a thousand pieces of glass in a single lampshade.

The Lotus lamp is one of the most magnificent leaded shade/base combinations ever produced by Tiffany Studios. The lotus motif has its roots in Egyptian and Indian cultures, and for artists of the Art Nouveau movement in France the lotus represented rebirth. Only three examples of this well-balanced and harmonious work are known to still exist. The lamp has a bronze base covered with finely detailed mosaic tiles of vibrant green. At the top the stalk branches into 20 bronze stems. The top eight stems end in light bulbs covered with blown shades of shimmering Favrile glass, giving the impression of barely-opened lotus buds in radiant pink and soft white. The lower stems hold a leaded glass shade representing lotus flowers in full bloom rendered in pink, orange, and red against a backdrop of striking green leaves. This magnificent lamp aptly displays Tiffany's great love of nature and his genius in vividly interpreting it. It was sold in December 1997 at Christie's auction house in New York for $2,807,500—a record price for a Tiffany lamp. Even at the time it was made, the Lotus lamp was very difficult to produce, and at $750 (in 1906), was Tiffany's most expensive model. Indeed, the studio produced just one Lotus lamp at a time, beginning production of another example only when the prior one had been sold. Other lamps of similar

Umgebung ihrer Häuser und Wohnungen an der Schönheit der Favrile-Gläser erfreuen. Die meisten Lampen zeigen Blumenmotive in einer scheinbar grenzenlosen Farbpalette, einige weisen jedoch auch geometrische Formen auf. Die Füße sind meist aus Metall gefertigt und können mit jedem beliebigen Lampenschirmmodell kombiniert werden; nur manchmal ist ein Fuß auf einen bestimmten Lampenschirm zugeschnitten. Niemand kann mit Gewissheit sagen, wie viele Lampen insgesamt produziert wurden. In einem Katalog von 1906 zum Beispiel wurden jedoch mehr als 300 verschiedene Modelle angeboten.

Der Preis für eine Lampe durchschnittlicher Größe betrug zu Beginn des 20. Jahrhunderts 100 Dollar, kleinere Lampen wurden schon ab 40 Dollar angeboten. Lampen, Vasen und andere Objekte aus Tiffanys Werkstätten waren Luxusartikel, auf die kein wohlhabender, prestigebewusster Amerikaner verzichten wollte. In Europa wurden sie von Siegfried Bing in seiner Pariser Galerie vertrieben. Obwohl die meisten seiner Kunden aus den wohlhabendsten amerikanischen Familien stammten und seine Arbeiten für die damalige Zeit sehr teuer waren, war Tiffany davon überzeugt, dass ein Heim auch mit wenig Geld schön eingerichtet werden könne. 1910 sagte er dazu: »Verschwendung bringt keine Schönheit hervor, und wie einige arme Leute haben auch viele sehr Reiche den Wert des guten Geschmacks noch nicht erkannt. Oft schiebt das Geld dem guten Geschmack sogar einen Riegel vor, weil es zu Protzertum und Prunksucht verführt.«

Tiffanys Lampen können in verschiedene Kategorien unterteilt werden: Es gibt einfache und komplexe, kleine und große, schlichte und aufwendig gestaltete. Es gibt Lampen in der Form von Kegeln oder Kugeln, Tisch-, Steh- und Hängelampen, darunter die Modelle, die Tiffany als »hängende Bouquets« bezeichnete. Unter heutigen Sammlern besonders gefragt sind jedoch die vielen »Blumenlampen« mit ihren charakteristischen, reich – manchmal auch mit Glasmosaiken – verzierten Bronzefüßen. Tiffany ließ sich für seine Lampenschirme von vielen verschiedenen Blumen inspirieren: Geranien, Mohnblumen, Klematis, Weihnachtssternen, Wasserlilien, Osterglocken, Tulpen, Pfingstrosen, Kapuzinerkresse, Narzissen, Magnolien, Begonien, Hortensien, Goldregen, Rosen und Apfelblüten. Außerdem finden sich Blauregen, Weinstock-, Kirschbaum- und Bambusblattmotive sowie exotische Früchte wie etwa Ananas

Parmi les lampes Tiffany, se trouvent plusieurs variétés, simples ou complexes, petites ou grandes, sans artifices ou somptueusement élaborées. Certaines sont en forme de cône ou de globe. Il y a des lampes de table, des lampadaires et des lampes suspendues (Tiffany nomme certains modèles « bouquets suspendus »). Toutefois, ce sont surtout les innombrables lampes florales, avec leur fameux pied en bronze ciselé, parfois incrusté de mosaïques de verre, qui sont aujourd'hui recherchées par les collectionneurs. Parmi les innombrables fleurs qui ont parsemé ses abat-jour, on reconnaît le géranium, le coquelicot, la clématite, le nénuphar, la jonquille, la tulipe, la pivoine, la capucine, le narcisse, le magnolia, le bégonia, l'hortensia, le cytise, la rose, la fleur de pommier, de cerisier et la feuille de bambou. On trouve aussi de la glycine et des fruits exotiques comme l'ananas. Certains styles d'abat-jour rappellent des périodes historiques célèbres, comme les modèles élisabéthain, vénitien ou russe. Son

Page from a catalog for bronze lamps issued by Tiffany Studios.

Seite aus einem Bronzelampen-Katalog, herausgegeben von den Tiffany Studios.

Page d'un catalogue des lampes en bronze, publié par les Tiffany Studios.

c. 1913. Courtesy Alastair Duncan, NY.

complexity and cost were the Cobweb and the Butterfly, each listed at $500, while the Wisteria and Pond Lily models were priced at $400.

Another Tiffany lamp recently sold at auction is the Peacock centerpiece table lamp, sold in December 1998 by Phillips in New York for $1,872,500. This spectacular lamp, the only one of its kind known to exist, is a masterful combination of shade and gilded bronze base. Although the peacock motif is characteristic of Art Nouveau, it is rare among Tiffany lamps. Rows of peacock feathers adorn the glass shade, beautifully complementing the heart and scallop shapes of the bronze and glass base. Experts believe that Tiffany commissioned the lamp for his own luxurious residence on 72nd Street and Madison Avenue in New York, which also served as a showroom.

There is no doubt that Tiffany's lamps were designed and assembled by highly trained artisans and superb colorists. Tiffany left the designing of most of the lamps and their bases to the artists working for him; however, every design needed his final approval before it could be put into large-scale production. In 1892, long before women's suffrage in the United States, Tiffany hired his first group of women artisans to work in Tiffany Studios. Two years later he was employing some 50 women. In 1904, Clara Driscoll, one of Tiffany's designers, was said to be the highest paid woman in America at a time when women earned on average 60% less than men. Tiffany had always believed that employing women would ensure a higher quality of artistry in his creations. Yet when Candace Wheeler, his partner in L. C. Tiffany & Associated Artists, insisted on receiving credit for her designs, Tiffany dissolved the company and decreed that all designers should work under the business name of Louis C. Tiffany Co. Nevertheless, Clara Driscoll received individual recognition for her Dragonfly lampshade, which won first prize in the 1900 Paris Exhibition.

Most of the thousands of lamps produced by Tiffany Studios were signed "Tiffany Studios, New York," some-

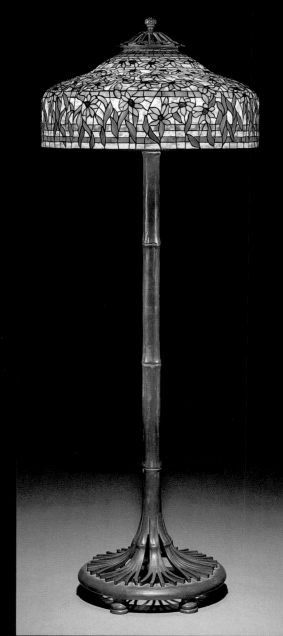

Black-eyed Susan floor lamp with bronze base.

Stehlampe mit Bronzefuß und Rudbeckiadekor.

Lampadaire Rudbeckia avec un pied de bronze.

h: 171 cm, ø 62.2 cm. Courtesy Art Focus, Zurich.

elisabethanischen, den venezianischen, den russischen und den Empirestil auf. Ungemein beliebt waren auch die Libellen-Lampenschirme (»Dragonfly«) mit ihren schillernden Farben, die in vielen verschiedenen Größen und Formen hergestellt wurden. Manche der komplexeren Lampenschirme setzen sich aus mehr als 1000 Glasstücken zusammen.

Die Lotos-Lampe gehört zu den spektakulärsten und prachtvollsten Kombinationen aus einem bleiverglasten Lampenschirm und einem darauf abgestimmten Lampenfuß, die je in den Tiffany-Studios gefertigt wurden. Das Lotosmotiv hat seine Wurzeln in der ägyptischen und in der indischen Kultur. Für die französischen Art-Nouveau-Künstler repräsentierte die Lotosblume die Wiedergeburt. Von diesem ausgewogenen und harmonischen Lampenmodell sind nur noch zwei Exemplare bekannt. Der Bronzefuß mit seinem detailreichen Mosaikbesatz in pulsierendem Grün verzweigt sich am oberen Rand in 20 Lotosblumenstängel. Die oberen acht Stängel münden in Lampenschirme aus geblasenem schimmerndem Favrile-Glas, die den Eindruck von sich öffnenden Lotosblüten in kraftvollen rosa und sanften weißen Farbtönen entstehen lassen. Die unteren Stängel halten einen bleiverglasten Lampenschirm, der in Rosa, Orange und Rot wiedergegebene Lotosblumen in voller Blüte vor dem Hintergrund sattgrüner Blätter zeigt. In dieser faszinierenden Lampe hat Tiffany seine Liebe zur Schönheit der Natur auf unvergleichlich geniale Art und Weise zum Ausdruck gebracht. Im Dezember 1997 erzielte sie auf einer Auktion bei Christie's in New York 2 807 500 Dollar – ein Rekordpreis für eine Tiffany-Lampe. Für die Herstellung der Lotos-Lampe war ein außergewöhnlich großer Arbeitsaufwand erforderlich, und sie war 1906 mit 750 Dollar Tiffanys teuerstes Modell. Tatsächlich wurde immer nur jeweils eine Lotos-Lampe hergestellt; die nächste wurde erst dann in Angriff genommen, wenn die Vorgängerin verkauft worden war. Andere, ähnlich komplexe und kostspielige Lampenmodelle waren »Spinnennetz« (»Cobweb«) und »Schmetterling« (»Butterfly«), die für jeweils 500 Dollar angeboten wurden, während die Modelle »Blauregen« (»Wistaria«) und »Teichlilie« (»Pond Lily«) für jeweils 400 Dollar verkauft wurden.

Im Dezember 1998 wurde die prachtvolle Tafelaufsatz-lampe »Pfau« (»Peacock«) vom Auktionshaus Phillips in

abat-jour « Libellule » connaît un immense succès et est produit dans toute une gamme de formes, de tailles et de couleurs. Certains abat-jour, parmi les plus complexes, comportent chacun plus d'un millier d'éléments de verre.

La lampe « Lotus » est l'un des ensembles socle/abat-jour en mosaïque de verre les plus splendides et les plus spectaculaires jamais produits par les ateliers Tiffany. Le motif du lotus trouve ses racines dans les civilisations indienne et égyptienne et pour les artistes français de l'Art Nouveau, le lotus est symbole de renaissance. Il ne subsiste aujourd'hui que deux spécimens de ce modèle harmonieux et si finement équilibré. La lampe repose sur un pied en bronze, orné d'un relief de mosaïques vert vif finement ouvragé. Le haut du fût se divise en vingt branches. Les huit branches supérieures sont surmontées d'ampoules protégées par des abat-jour soufflés de verre Favrile chatoyant, évoquant des bourgeons de lotus à peine éclos, rose vif et blanc crémeux. Les branches inférieures portent un abat-jour en mosaïque de verre représentant des fleurs de lotus largement épanouies, colorées de rose, orange et rouge, sur un fond de feuilles vert profond. Cette incroyable lampe est un parfait exemple de l'extraordinaire amour que Tiffany portait à la nature et de son génie pour l'interpréter avec éclat. En décembre 1997 elle est vendue chez Christie's, à New York, pour la somme de 2 807 500 dollars, prix record pour une lampe Tiffany. Même à l'époque de sa fabrication, la lampe Lotus était très difficile à produire et son prix, 750 dollars en 1906, faisait d'elle le modèle le plus cher des Ateliers. De fait, on n'y produit alors qu'une seule lampe « Lotus » à la fois, et on ne commence la fabrication d'un nouvel exemplaire que lorsque le précédent a été vendu. Il existe d'autres lampes d'une semblable complexité et d'un prix aussi élevé comme la « Toile d'araignée » et le « Papillon », chacune mise au prix de 500 dollars, alors que la « Glycine » et le « Nénuphar » sont vendues à 400 dollars.

Autre lampe remarquable, la fabuleuse « Paon », ornement de centre de table, vendue aux enchères à New York par Phillips, en décembre 1998 pour 1 872 500 dollars. Unique en son genre, elle est d'une beauté saisissante, équilibre magistral entre son abat-jour et son pied en bronze doré. Quoique caractéristique de l'Art Nouveau, le motif du paon est très rare dans les lampes Tiffany. Des rangées de plumes de paon ornent l'abat-jour et viennent

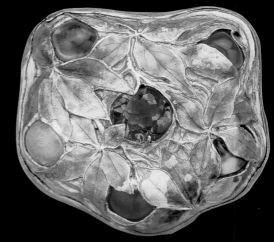

times with a number identifying the style of the lamp. The word "Favrile" is also occasionally found. According to the late Dr. Egon Neustadt, who owned one of the largest collections of Tiffany lamps in the world, "another figure code is sometimes found: this, known as a dash number, is reputedly the private cipher used by the studios to mark those lamp shades Tiffany thought to be exceptional." In some cases the stamped seal of Tiffany Studios appears on the bronze base of the lamp; in others it is etched into the glass of the Favrile shades. It is common to find no signature at all on certain models of small shades. Experts say the kind of glass used for the shade is the best proof of its

New York für 1 872 500 Dollar versteigert – der zweithöchste Preis, der bis heute für eine Tiffany-Lampe erreicht wurde. Diese wahrhaft einzigartige Lampe – ein Pendant ist nicht bekannt – stellt ebenfalls eine meisterhafte Kombination aus einem Lampenschirm und einem vergoldeten Bronzefuß dar. Für die französische Art-Nouveau-Bewegung war der Pfau ein charakteristisches Motiv, von Tiffany wurde es jedoch nur selten für seine Lampen verwendet. Die den gläsernen Lampenschirm schmückenden Pfauenfederreihen sind wunderbar auf die Herz- und Muschelformen des aus Bronze und Glas gearbeiteten Fußes abgestimmt. Diese Lampe ließ Tiffany vermutlich für sein luxuriöses Wohnhaus an der 72nd Street/Madison Avenue in Manhattan fertigen, das ihm auch zu Ausstellungszwecken diente.

Tiffanys Lampen wurden von vorzüglich ausgebildeten Fachkräften und hervorragenden Koloristen gestaltet und zusammengesetzt. Tiffany ließ die meisten Lampenschirme und -füße von den Künstlern entwerfen, die für ihn arbeiteten, doch jeder Entwurf musste von ihm selbst gebilligt werden, bevor er in die Produktion ging. 1892, lange bevor die Frauen in den Vereinigten Staaten das Wahlrecht bekamen, stellte Tiffany die ersten Kunsthandwerkerinnen ein. Zwei Jahre später beschäftigte er schon etwa 50 Frauen, und 1904 galt Clara Driscoll, die als Gestalterin für Tiffany arbeitete, als die am höchsten bezahlte Frau in Amerika. Frauen verdienten damals 60 % weniger als männliche Arbeitskräfte. Tiffany glaubte, dass Frauen die Qualität seiner Kreationen besser gewährleisten konnten als Männer. Als jedoch Candace Wheeler, seine Partnerin in der Firma Louis C. Tiffany & Associated Artists, auf ihrem Urheberrecht an ihren Entwürfen bestand, löste Tiffany diese Firma auf und verfügte, dass künftig alle Entwürfe seiner Designer unter dem neuen Firmennamen Louis C. Tiffany Co. zusammengefasst werden sollten. Clara Driscoll fand jedoch trotzdem die ihr gebührende Anerkennung für ihren Libellen-Lampenschirm (»Dragonfly«), der auf der Pariser Weltausstellung des Jahres 1900 mit dem ersten Preis ausgezeichnet wurde.

Die meisten der vielen Tausend Lampen, die in den Tiffany-Werkstätten gefertigt wurden, tragen die Signatur »Tiffany Studios New York«, manchmal mit einer Nummer, die das Lampenmodell bezeichnete. Auch das Wort »Favrile« ist gelegentlich zu finden. Egon Neustadt zufolge, der eine

souligner avec élégance les formes de cœur et de coquilles du socle en verre et en bronze. Selon certains experts, Tiffany aurait commandé cette lampe lui-même pour sa luxueuse résidence, à l'angle de 72e Street et de Madison Avenue, à New York, qui lui servait aussi de salle d'exposition.

Il ne fait aucun doute que le dessin et l'assemblage des lampes Tiffany sont l'œuvre d'artisans hautement compétents et de coloristes sans égal. Tiffany confiait la conception de la plupart des lampes et de leurs pieds aux artistes engagés par lui-même. Toutefois, chaque projet devait obtenir son approbation finale avant de suivre la filière de production à grande échelle. En 1892, bien avant le droit de vote des femmes aux Etats-Unis, Tiffany engage dans ses Ateliers sa première équipe de femmes artisans. Deux ans plus tard, elles sont une cinquantaine. En 1904, Clara Driscoll, l'une de ses dessinatrices, est réputée pour être la femme la mieux payée d'Amérique, à une époque où les femmes gagnent en moyenne 60% de moins que les hommes. Tiffany a toujours pensé qu'employer des femmes, assurerait à ses créations une meilleure qualité artistique. Toutefois, quand Candace Wheeler, son associée à la L. C. Tiffany & Associated Artists, insiste pour signer ses propres créations, Tiffany dissout la société et décrète que tous les concepteurs-maquettistes doivent se ranger sous l'appellation Louis C. Tiffany Co. Cependant, Clara Driscoll est personnellement distinguée pour sa lampe « Libellule » qui remporte un premier prix à l'Exposition Universelle de Paris, en 1900.

La plupart des lampes produites aux Ateliers sont signées «Tiffany Studios, New York», parfois avec un numéro d'identification du style. Le nom « Favrile » apparaît à l'occasion. Selon le Dr Egon Neustadt, propriétaire d'une des plus importantes collections de lampes Tiffany au monde, il existe parfois un autre code chiffré, appelé code à tiret, utilisé semble-t-il pour signaler ces abat-jour que Tiffany jugeait exceptionnels. Dans certains cas, le cachet portant la signature Tiffany apparaît sur le pied en bronze de la lampe, dans d'autres, il est gravé dans l'abat-jour en Favrile. Il n'est pas rare de ne trouver aucune signature, sur certains modèles d'abat-jour de petite taille. Selon les experts, la qualité du verre utilisé pour l'abat-jour est la meilleure preuve de son authenticité, et pour le Dr Neustadt, tout motif connu est, à l'évidence, une indication

authenticity. As Dr. Neustadt said, "an established design is, of course, another indication that the shade is genuine ... [and] in the case of a Favrile shade, authenticity may be determined by the quality of the glass and by the etched initials." At the peak of Tiffany's career, about 30,000 items—most of them lampshades—were produced each year. Another proof of their success, both artistically and financially, is the extent to which they were imitated: Copies sprouted everywhere, like mushrooms after a rain.

Vases, jewelry and "fancy goods": Nature becomes art

Favrile glass is distinguished by ... brilliant or deeply toned colors, usually iridescent like the wings of certain American butterflies, the necks of pigeons and peacocks, the wing covers of various beetles.

Glass was at the heart of Tiffany's activities from the 1880's on. In 1898 he published his fifth booklet listing examples of his Favrile glass, and tracing the history of its development back to 3064 BC [!] in Egypt. Surprisingly, this publication also listed all the museums worldwide that owned Tiffany glass at that time. If this disclosure was meant to impress other museums and private buyers, it was certainly successful. Early collectors of Tiffany glass included the Metropolitan Museum of Art in New York, the Imperial Museum in Tokyo and the Smithsonian Insti-

The Briars, Tiffany's summer home on Long Island prior to construction of Laurelton Hall.

The Briars, Tiffanys Sommerdomizil auf Long Island vor dem Bau von Laurelton Hall.

The Briars, résidence d'été de Tiffany à Long Island avant la construction de Laurelton Hall.

c. 1900. Courtesy Alastair Duncan, NY.

A Tiffany Studios logo.

Logo der Tiffany Studios.

Logo des Tiffany Studios.

c. 1905. Private collection.

tution in Washington D.C. as well as museums in Paris, Berlin, Hamburg, Melbourne, Dublin, Vienna, St. Petersburg, and many other collections throughout Europe. Tiffany continued to publish brochures and lists of his works over the years, as did museums that either purchased his creations or received them as donations from patrons. Tiffany also had an elaborate and elegant showroom in New York in which he was able to exhibit and present his works.

der größten Sammlungen von Tiffany-Lampen besitzt, ist in einigen Fällen »ein zusätzlicher, als ›Strichnummer‹ bekannter Zahlencode zu finden, der, wie man annehmen darf, die Lampenschirme bezeichnet, die Tiffany für außergewöhnlich hielt«. In einigen Fällen wurde die Signatur »Tiffany Studios/New York« in den Bronzefuß eingestempelt, in anderen in das Glas der Lampenschirme eingeätzt. Auf kleineren Lampenmodellen ist gewöhnlich keine Signatur zu finden. In diesen Fällen lässt sich Experten zufolge die Authentizität am ehesten anhand der Qualität des Glases bestimmen. Egon Neustadt dazu: »Ein zweifelsfrei Tiffany zuzuschreibender Entwurf ist natürlich ein weiterer Hinweis auf die Echtheit eines Lampenschirms … Im Falle eines Favrile-Lampenschirms kann die Authentizität anhand der Qualität des Glases und durch die eingeätzten Initialen ermittelt werden.« In den Spitzenjahren wurden in den Tiffany-Studios jährlich etwa 30 000 Objekte – hauptsächlich Lampenschirme – produziert. Der beste Beweis für den künstlerischen und finanziellen Erfolg gerade auch der Lampenschirme war die Tatsache, dass der Markt mit Imitationen regelrecht überschwemmt wurde.

Natur wird zur Kunst:
Glasvasen und Objekte aus sonstigen Materialien

Favrile-Glas zeichnet sich durch … brillante oder intensive, zumeist irisierende Farben aus – wie die Flügel mancher amerikanischer Schmetterlinge, Tauben- und Pfauenhälse, die Deckflügel verschiedener Käfer. (Louis Comfort Tiffany)

Seit den 1880er-Jahren stand Glas im Zentrum von Tiffanys Aktivitäten. 1898 veröffentlichte er seine fünfte Broschüre mit Beispielen seines Favrile-Glases. Darin führte er die Geschichte der Glaskunst auf das Jahr 3064 v. Chr. in Ägypten zurück und listete sämtliche Museen in aller Welt auf, die damals Tiffany-Gläser besaßen. Dazu gehörten das Metropolitan Museum of Art in New York, das Kaiserliche Museum in Tokio, die Smithsonian Institution in Washington, D.C., und mehr als zwei Dutzend Sammlungen in ganz Europa. Diese beeindruckende Liste verfehlte ihre Wirkung auf andere Museen und Privatsammler nicht. In späteren Broschüren konnte Tiffany diese Liste ständig erweitern. Viele seiner Arbeiten wurden von Museen angekauft oder gestiftet. Seit 1906 präsentierte Tiffany die in

supplémentaire que l'abat-jour est authentique, dans le cas d'un abat-jour Favrile, l'authenticité peut être déterminée par la qualité du verre et les initiales gravées. Au summum de sa période créative, environ 30 000 objets, pour la plupart des abat-jour, sont manufacturés chaque année. La meilleure preuve du succès des lampes, tant sur le plan artistique que financier, est la quantité d'imitations qu'elles engendrent alors. Les copies surgissent de partout, comme les champignons après la pluie.

La nature devient art:
vases de verre et œuvres en diverses matières

Le verre Favrile se distingue par des couleurs vives ou profondes, généralement irisées comme les ailes de certains papillons américains, la gorge des pigeons et des paons ou la surface des ailes de divers scarabées. (Louis Comfort Tiffany)

A partir de 1880, le verre est au centre des activités de Tiffany. En 1898, il publie sa cinquième plaquette présentant la liste de ses verres Favrile et retraçant l'histoire de ce matériau jusqu'en 3064 avant J-C, en Egypte. Curieusement, on trouve aussi dans cette plaquette la liste de tous les musées du monde qui possèdent, à l'époque, des verres Tiffany. Si le but est ainsi d'impressionner les autres musées et les acheteurs privés, c'est à n'en point douter un succès. Parmi les premiers acquéreurs, on trouve le Metropolitan Museum of Art, le musée Impérial de Tokyo, la Smithsonian Institution de Washington D.C., et plus d'une cinquantaine d'autres collections dans toute l'Europe. Au cours des années, Tiffany continue à publier des brochures et des listes de ses œuvres, comme le font les musées qui achètent ses créations ou les reçoivent de généreux donateurs. A New York, Tiffany possède aussi une élégante salle d'exposition d'un goût raffiné où il peut montrer et mettre en valeur ses œuvres.

Dans le domaine du verre, la créativité de Tiffany ne se limite pas aux vitraux et aux abat-jour. En fait, ses vases et autres récipients d'apparat comptent parmi ses articles les plus populaires et les plus accessibles financièrement. Ce sont aussi les objets les plus proches des verreries de l'Art Nouveau, produites en Europe par son contemporain Emile Gallé et les autres artistes de l'Ecole dite de Nancy, qui participent aux salons français entre 1895 et 1905. Les

Tiffany's creativity in glass was not limited to stained glass windows and lampshades. In fact, his vases and other vessels fashioned in glass rank among the most popular and affordable objects he ever created. They are also the items in his oeuvre that most closely resemble the Art Nouveau glass being produced in Europe by his contemporary Emile Gallé and other artists of the School of Nancy that were displayed in the French salons from 1895 to 1905. Galle's designs were also inspired by nature; however, unlike Tiffany he did not use bright colors. After creating transparent glass decorated with enamel paint, Galle went on to produce opaque glass. He began by experimenting with metallic oxides, as Tiffany had done, but Galle further decorated his glass objects with engravings. Galle, who died of leukemia in 1904, was more famous than Tiffany in Europe at the time.

Tiffany's talents as a great colorist, designer, and naturalist are clearly apparent in the many hundreds of styles of wares he developed in Favrile glass, spanning a haunting rainbow of colors. The forms of these objects were inspired by a variety of sources: ancient Greek, Roman, Chinese and Islamic glass, English tableware in glass and porcelain, and elegant floral forms were but a few of them. Tiffany promoted and sold his glass tableware through his own catalogues and brochures, and through S. Bing, his exclusive European dealer up until the latter's death. Bing sold numerous Tiffany vases to European private collections, and to museums in London, Paris, Berlin, Tokyo, Copenhagen and many other capitals. One of the most outstanding collections of Tiffany's portable glassware is in the Metropolitan Museum of Art in New York, donated by the Havemeyer family and by Tiffany himself. This remarkable collection contains at least one example of every style Tiffany produced between 1897 and 1913.

Tiffany was also able to create masterfully with colored glass on a large scale. He produced mosaic murals such as the *Dream Garden* of 1915, a work measuring approximately 5.25 x 4.6 meters, commissioned for the marble lobby of the Curtis Publishing Company in Philadelphia. The mural is based on a painting by the American artist Maxfield Parrish, and is the second largest mosaic Tiffany ever made. He also designed a glass curtain representing the Mexican landscape for the *Palacio de Bellas Artes* in Mexico.

---

schen Werkstätten gefertigten Objekten in großzügigen und eleganten Ausstellungsräumen an der Madison Avenue in New York.

Tiffanys Kreativität mit Glas war nicht auf Buntglasfenster und Lampenschirme beschränkt. Zu seinen beliebtesten und auch erschwinglicheren Objekten gehören seine Vasen und Gefäße aus Glas. In seinem Œuvre stellen die Vasen zudem die Objekte dar, die eine besonders enge Verwandtschaft mit dem europäischen Jugendstil zeigen: Émile Gallé und andere Künstler der so genannten Schule von Nancy schufen ähnliche Glasobjekte, die von 1895 bis 1905 in den französischen Salons vorgestellt wurden. Wie Tiffany ließ auch Gallé sich von der Natur inspirieren; er setzte allerdings andere Akzente und bevorzugte gedämpftere Farben. Von mit Emailfarbe verziertem transparentem Glas ging er später zu undurchsichtigem Glas über. Wie Tiffany begann auch er mit Metalloxiden zu experimentieren. Anders als Tiffany jedoch versah Gallé seine Glasobjekte mit eingravierten Verzierungen. Gallé, der im Jahr 1904 an Leukämie starb, war seinerzeit in Europa bekannter als Tiffany.

Seine schier zahllosen Gefäße aus Favrile-Glas in aller erdenklichen Formen und Regenbogenfarben führen uns Tiffanys Begabungen als Kolorist, Gestalter und Naturalist immer wieder vor Augen. Inspiriert wurden sie von den verschiedensten Quellen: alten griechischen, römischen, chinesischen und islamischen Gläsern, englischem Glas und Porzellangeschirr und eleganten Blumenformen, um nur einige zu nennen. Auch die Glasgefäße wurden über Kataloge und Broschüren vertrieben. Siegfried Bing, sein europäischer Repräsentant, verkaufte viele davon an Privatsammlungen und Museen in Paris, Berlin, London, Tokio, Kopenhagen und anderen Städten. Das Museum o Modern Art in New York besitzt eine der bestsortierten Sammlungen, bestehend aus zwischen 1897 und 1913 entstandenen Vasen und Glasgefäßen, die durch Schenkungen der Familie Havemeyer und von Tiffany selbs zusammengetragen wurde.

Auch im großen Format konnte Tiffany seine Meisterschaft als Glaskünstler unter Beweis stellen. Er entwar zum Beispiel Wandmosaiken wie »The Dream Garden« (»Der Traumgarten«; 1915, 15,24 x 4,57 m) für die Marmorlobby des Verlagsgebäudes der Curtis Publishing Co in Philadelphia. »The Dream Garden« beruht auf einem

dessins de Gallé s'inspirent aussi de la nature, mais, à la
différence de Tiffany, il ne se sert pas de couleurs vives.
Après avoir créé le verre transparent, à décor de peinture
émaillée, Gallé se met à fabriquer des verreries opaques.
Pour ses premières expériences, il recourt aux oxydes métalliques, comme l'avait fait Tiffany, mais ajoute à ses verreries un décor gravé. Gallé, qui meurt de leucémie en
1904, jouit à son époque, d'une plus grande renommée en
Europe que Tiffany.

Bronze mounted mosaic Favrile glass mantle clock.
Kaminuhr aus Favrilglas-Mosaik in Bronzemontierung.
Pendule en mosaïque de verre Favrile avec une sertissure de bronze.
h: 29.8 cm. c. 1910. Christie's Images.

Glassware created by Emile Gallé.
Glasobjekte, entworfen von Emile Gallé.
Objets de verre réalisées par Emile Gallé. Christie's Images.

City in 1911. His inventive ideas continually produced fascinating and inspiring masterpieces that transformed colored glass into the brilliant colors of nature, eliciting ever new and glowing shades from simple daylight.

Enamel work by Tiffany Studios came about as an extension of his works in glass. His experiments began in 1898 when he first layered glass with gold or silver foil to create a translucent effect. The enamels were first shown publicly at the 1900 *Exposition Universelle Internationale* in Paris and by all accounts were very well received. However, only 750 enamel pieces were ever produced, leading to the closure of this department by 1910, although production resumed for a brief period around 1920.

Tiffany's studios entered into field of jewelry design only in 1902, after the death of his father, when Louis C. Tiffany became vice president and artistic director of Tiffany & Co. He was familiar with the design of jewelry, as he had collaborated on some pieces for his father's display in the 1900 exposition in Paris. Tiffany Studios produced necklaces, brooches and other forms of jewelry, which were displayed in 1904 at the St. Louis International Exposition in Missouri. He used semiprecious stones in his jewelry work, in contrast to the precious stones used by Tiffany & Co., but placed them in a totally new and inventive manner, even combining them with enamels. In keeping with his signature love of nature, Tiffany's primary jewelry motifs were of plants and insects.

Tiffany Studios also produced objects in copper and bronze such as desk sets, candelabrae, boxes, inkwells and picture frames that were marketed through a special catalogue. The metalwork received international exposure when a selection was shown at London's Grafton Galleries in 1899, an exhibition arranged by S. Bing. Most of the metalwork designs (collectively called "fancy goods" in his catalogues) were inspired by nature, with glass occasionally used to accentuate the bronze. The desk sets were offered either with a green patina or plated in gold.

For a short period between 1904 and 1910, Tiffany produced and sold ceramic pieces, but discontinued them in all likelihood because of intense competition from other, more established art pottery manufacturers such as Grueby and Rookwood. Though Tiffany's pieces were never very popular with the public, they are now prized by collectors for their relative rarity.

Gemälde des amerikanischen Künstlers Maxfield Parrish und gilt als das zweitgrößte Mosaik der Welt. 1911 entwarf er für den Palacio de Bellas Artes in Mexiko-Stadt einen gläsernen Vorhang, der eine mexikanische Landschaft zeigt. Bereits 1909 hatte er nach einer Vorlage des Malers Harry Stoner einen 1911 fertig gestellten Glasmosaikvorhang für das Nationaltheater von Mexiko-Stadt entworfen, der ebenfalls eine mexikanische Landschaft zeigt. Seine Ideen brachten immer wieder faszinierende, verblüffende und inspirierende Meisterwerke hervor, die die leuchtenden Farben der Natur in Glas wiedergeben und das Tageslicht in immer neuen Farben zum Leuchten bringen.

Von der Glas- zur Emailkunst war es für Tiffany nur ein kleiner Schritt. Seine Experimente mit Email begannen 1898, als er zum ersten Mal Glas mit Gold- oder Silberfolie belegte, um einen lichtdurchlässigen Effekt zu erreichen. Als seine Emailarbeiten auf der Pariser Weltausstellung von 1900 erstmals gezeigt wurden, stießen sie auf großes Interesse. Dennoch wurden alles in allem nur 750 Emailobjekte gefertigt. 1910 schloss die Emailwerkstatt der Tiffany-Studios, deren Produktion Tiffany um 1920 noch einmal für kurze Zeit wieder aufnahm.

Erst 1902, nach dem Tod seines Vaters, trat Tiffany als künstlerischer Direktor und Vizepräsident in dessen Unternehmen ein. Schon in früheren Jahren hatte er gemeinsam mit seinem Vater an einigen Stücken gearbeitet, die auf der Pariser Weltausstellung von 1900 gezeigt worden waren. 1904 waren die von ihm entworfenen Halsketten, Broschen und andere Schmuckgegenstände Teil der Weltausstellung in St. Louis. Häufig verwendete er Pflanzen- und Insektenmotive, und er führte zusätzlich zu den althergebrachten Edelsteinen Halbedelsteine und auch Email in seine Entwürfe ein.

In den Tiffany-Studios wurden auch Kupfer- und Bronze-Objekte wie Schreibtischgarnituren, Kandelaber, Schatullen, Bilderrahmen und Tintenfässer produziert, die fast alle von der Natur inspiriert worden waren und in einem Spezialkatalog als »fancy goods« (Geschenkartikel) angeboten wurden. Eine Auswahl von Metallarbeiten zeigte 1899 eine von Siegfried Bing organisierte Ausstellung in den Grafton Galleries in London. Gelegentlich wurden die Bronzeobjekte mit Glaselementen akzentuiert. Die Schreibtischgarnituren waren mit einer grünen Patina versehen oder vergoldet.

L'immense talent de Tiffany comme coloriste, dessinateur et naturaliste apparaît nettement dans les centaines de styles d'objets de vaisselle qu'il crée en verre Favrile, déployant un véritable arc-en-ciel de couleurs fascinantes. Pour les formes, les sources d'inspiration sont diverses : verres antiques grecs et romains, verreries chinoises et islamiques ; vaisselle anglaise, en verre et porcelaine ; élégantes formes florales, pour n'en citer que quelques-unes. Tiffany expose et vend sa vaisselle de verre au moyen de ses catalogues et brochures et par l'entremise de son marchand exclusif en Europe, S. Bing, qui le restera jusqu'à sa mort. Bing vend nombre de vases à des collections privées en Europe et à des musées de Paris, Berlin, Londres, Tokyo, Copenhague et bien d'autres capitales. Une des plus belles collections se trouve au Metropolitan Museum de New York, don de la famille Havemeyer et de Tiffany lui-même. Cette collection remarquable contient au moins un exemplaire de chacun des styles créés par Tiffany entre 1897 et 1913.

Tiffany sait aussi réaliser de grands décors de verre de couleurs. Il produit des mosaïques murales comme le « Dream Garden/Jardin de rêve » de 1915, destiné au vestibule en marbre des Editions Curtis, à Philadelphie, et mesurant 15 sur 5 mètres. Inspirée d'un tableau de l'Américain Maxfield Parrish, la fresque est considérée comme l'une des plus grandes mosaïques du monde. En 1911, Tiffany crée aussi un rideau de verre, pour le Palacio de Bellas Artes de Mexico, représentant un paysage mexicain. Mêlant passion et créativité, il produit des chefs-d'œuvre impressionnants et exaltants, qui fixent à tout jamais les couleurs magiques de la nature dans le verre, illuminant le jour de jeux de lumière sans cesse renouvelés.

Ses émaux constituent une sorte d'extension de son travail du verre. Les premières expériences datent de 1898, quand il recouvre le verre de feuilles d'or ou d'argent afin de créer un effet translucide. Présentés pour la première fois à l'Exposition Universelle de Paris en 1900, les émaux sont fort bien reçus. Toutefois, il ne produira jamais que

Cover of The Art Work of Louis Comfort Tiffany. Only 502 copies of this book, written by art critic Charles De Kay with Tiffany's cooperation, were published in 1914 by request of Tiffany's children in order to record their father's accomplishments.

Einband von »The Art Work of Louis Comfort Tiffany«. Von diesem Buch, das der Kunstkritiker Charles De Kay unter Mitwirkung Tiffanys verfasste, wurden 1914 nur 502 Exemplare hergestellt. Das auf Wunsch von Tiffanys Kindern erstellte Opus sollte das Werk ihres Vaters verewigen.

Couverture du livre « The Art Work of Louis Comfort Tiffany ». Ce livre écrit par le critique d'art Charles de Kay en collaboration avec Tiffany ne fut publié en 1914 qu'à 502 exemplaires. Les enfants de Tiffany qui finançaient le projet voulaient immortaliser le nom leur père par cet ouvrage.

Courtesy Phillips Auctioneers, NY.

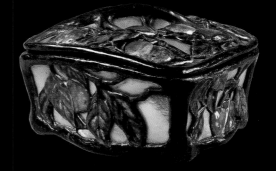

Enamel vessel with lid.

Emaillierte Dose.

Boîte émaillée avec couvercle.

c. 1898.

Tiffany designed his extravagant country estate, Laurelton Hall, which was completed in 1905, specifically in order to showcase his best work. Its 80 rooms were situated on nearly 600 acres overlooking Long Island Sound near Cold Spring Harbor, New York, and it was used primarily as a summer residence. The mansion incorporated a mixture of Islamic, Moorish, Oriental and other themes, and of course displayed Tiffany's glass windows, lamps, vases, mosaics, and even carpet designs. It is said that the estate's landscaping alone cost a million dollars.

Through the years Tiffany changed the name of his company several times. In 1885 the firm was incorporated as the Tiffany Glass Company, then in 1892, concurrent with the opening of the Corona glass factory, it became known as Tiffany Glass & Decorating. Around 1893 the glass division split into the Stourbridge Glass Company (for glassware) and the Allied Arts Company (for sheet glass), and in 1900 Allied Arts became Tiffany Studios. Tiffany Furnaces was added to the company roster in 1902 to produce

The front entrance loggia and bell-tower of Laurelton Hall.
(lot 277, part)

Favrile glassware in volume. When Tiffany retired from daily operations in 1919 (though he retained nominal control over the production lines), the non-glassware division was reorganized into the Tiffany Ecclesiastical Department, which still produced under the label Tiffany Studios. Tiffany Furnaces was dissolved in 1924. When Tiffany Studios officially declared bankruptcy in 1932—one year before Tiffany's death—the outstanding commis-

Laurelton Hall, Tiffany's showcase summer home. Front entrance and bell tower.

Laurelton Hall, Tiffanys repräsentatives Sommerdomizil. Haupteingang und Glockenturm.

Laurelton Hall, résidence d'été de Tiffany, une maison somptueuse. Entrée principale et clocher.

Christie's Images.

Zwischen 1904 und 1910 stellte Tiffany auch Keramik-Objekte her; da er mit anderen, etablierten Keramik-produzenten wie Grueby und Rookwood jedoch nicht kon-kurrieren konnte, wurde die Produktion nach wenigen Jahren wieder eingestellt. Aufgrund ihrer Seltenheit sind sie heute unter Sammlern sehr gefragt.

1905 wurde nach Tiffanys eigenen Plänen sein extra-vaganter Sommerlandsitz Laurelton Hall bei Cold Spring Harbor auf Long Island fertig gestellt. Das riesige Anwe-sen – ein Haus mit 80 Zimmern auf 580 Morgen Land – mit Blick auf den Long Island Sound stellte eine Mischung aus islamischen, maurischen, orientalischen und anderen Stilelementen dar und war mit Buntglasfenstern, Lampen, Vasen und Mosaiken aus seinen eigenen Werkstätten aus-gestattet. Allein für die Landschaftsgestaltung soll Tiffany 2 Mio. Dollar ausgegeben haben.

Im Laufe der Jahre änderte Tiffany mehrmals den Na-men seines Unternehmens. Aus der 1885 gegründeten Tif-fany Glass Company wurde 1892, zeitgleich mit der Er-öffnung der Glashütte in Corona, die Tiffany Glass & Decorating Company. Um 1893 wurde die Glasmanu-faktur in die Stourbridge Glass Company für die Hohl-glas- und die Allied Arts Company für die Flachglaspro-duktion aufgeteilt und 1900 die Allied Arts Company (Tiffany Glass & Decorating Company) in Tiffany Studios umbenannt. 1902 wurde dann noch die Glashütte Tiffany Furnaces gegründet, um Favrile-Glas in größeren Men-gen herstellen zu können, sowie im gleichen Jahr die Stourbridge Glass Company in Tiffany Furnaces umbe-nannt. 1919 zog sich Tiffany aus dem Alltagsbetrieb sei-ner Manufakturen zurück, blieb jedoch nominell für die einzelnen Produktionszweige verantwortlich. In diesem Jahr wurde sein Unternehmen in das Tiffany Ecclesiasti-cal Department, das weiterhin unter dem Namen Tiffany-Studios produzierte, und in die Tiffany Furnaces Inc. aufgeteilt. 1924 wurde die Tiffany Furnaces Inc. aufge-löst, und 1932 – ein Jahr vor Tiffanys Tod – meldeten die Tiffany-Studios Konkurs an. Die noch ausstehenden Auf-tragsarbeiten wurden von einer Gruppe ehemaliger Mit-arbeiter der Tiffany-Studios ausgeführt, die zu diesem Zweck die Westminster Memorial Studios gründeten. Auch aus diesen Namensänderungen geht hervor, dass Tiffany sein Unternehmen in einzelne »Werkstätten« mit jeweils auf bestimmte Bereiche spezialisierten Mitarbeitern orga-

750 pièces en émail, ce qui entraînera la fermeture de cette section en 1910, même si la production reprend brièvement autour de 1920.

Les Ateliers Tiffany ne commencent à s'intéresser à la création de joaillerie qu'à partir de 1902, après la mort du père, quand Louis C. Tiffany devient vice-président et directeur artistique de Tiffany & Co. Ayant collaboré à quelques pièces produites par son père pour l'Exposition de 1900 à Paris, Tiffany est déjà familiarisé à la conception de bijoux. Ses Ateliers vont réaliser des colliers, des broches et d'autres sortes de bijoux qui seront présentés à l'Expo-sition Internationale de St. Louis, dans le Missouri, en 1904. Contrairement aux habitudes de la Tiffany & Co, Tif-fany utilise des pierres semi-précieuses, mais il les dis-pose d'une manière nouvelle, totalement inventive, et les associe même à des émaux. Toujours fidèle à son amour inconditionnel de la nature, il met en scène, dans ses pre-miers émaux, des motifs de plantes et d'insectes.

Les Ateliers Tiffany produisent également des objets en cuivre et en bronze, comme des ensembles de bureau, des candélabres, des boîtes, des encadrements de tableaux et des encriers qui sont commercialisés sur catalogue spécia-lisé. Ces œuvres sur métal font leur apparition en 1899, lors d'une exposition aux Grafton Galleries de Londres, orga-nisée par S. Bing. Pour la plupart, ces créations sur métal (signalées dans ses catalogues sous la rubrique « produits fantaisie ») s'inspirent de la nature avec parfois des inser-tions de verre pour accentuer le bronze. Les ensembles de bureau sont proposés avec patine verte ou plaqués or.

Pendant une courte période, entre 1904 et 1910, Tiffa-ny manufacture et vend des objets de céramique, mais il finit par y renoncer, sans doute à cause de la forte concur-rence en provenance de faïenceries mieux établies, comme Grueby and Rookwood. Bien que peu appréciés par le pu-blic de l'époque, ces objets sont aujourd'hui fort re-cherchés des collectionneurs, du fait de leur rareté relative.

C'est Tiffany lui-même qui conçoit son extravagante demeure de Laurelton Hall, qui sera enfin terminée en 1905, et où il souhaite exposer ses plus belles œuvres. Les 80 salles s'étendent sur près de 240 hectares dominant le détroit de Long Island, près de Spring Harbor, état de New York. Il s'en sert d'abord comme résidence d'été. Le manoir offre un mélange de thèmes islamiques, maures-ques, orientaux et autres, et bien sûr, s'orne de vitraux

ions were completed by a group of Tiffany artisans under the name Westminster Memorial Studios. These name changes reflect Tiffany's organization of his production into "shops" and his recognition of the talent each design and production team brought to the company as a whole.

The man, the dream, and the legend

Infinite, endless labor makes the masterpiece.
Color is to the eye as music is to the ear. (L. C. T.)

According to people who knew him well, Tiffany was an eccentric, an autocratic, and a perfectionist. He was very demanding of his craftsmen, yet was also kind and generous to his many employees and demonstrated concern for their personal situations. The staff at Laurelton Hall respected him greatly, though not without a certain amount of trepidation, as did artisans at the studios, where he was known to walk down the lines with his cane and strike any piece that he found unacceptable. It is said that Tiffany would only allow a model to languish on a dealer's shelves for three months; after that he reclaimed it and offered it solely by catalogue, and if existing stock had not sold out within one year, he ceased production of that item entirely.

In his personal life, Tiffany was a family man who endured a number of tragedies. Two of his children died in infancy. His first wife, Mary Woodbridge Goddard, died in 1884 after 12 years of marriage leaving him three surviving children. In 1886 he married a distant cousin, Louise Wakeman Knox, with whom he had three additional

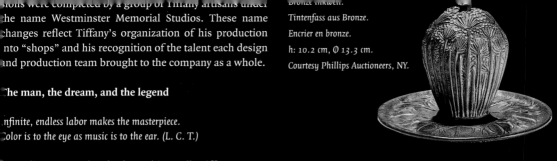

Bronze inkwell.
Tintenfass aus Bronze.
Encrier en bronze.
h: 10.2 cm, Ø 13.3 cm.
Courtesy Phillips Auctioneers, NY.

"My Family at Somesville." *Painting by Louis Comfort Tiffany, depicting his second wife, Louise, several of their children, and a nurse. Oil on canvas.*

»Meine Familie in Somesville«. *Gemälde von Louis Comfort Tiffany. Dargestellt sind Tiffanys zweite Frau, Louise, mehrere ihrer Kinder und ein Kindermädchen. Öl auf Leinwand.*

« Ma famille à Somesville ». *Ce tableau de Louis Comfort Tiffany montre sa seconde femme, Louise, plusieurs de leurs enfants et une bonne d'enfants. Huile sur toile.*

61 x 91,4 cm, c. 1888.
Collection of the Charles Hosmer Morse Museum of American Art, Winter Park, FL
© *The Charles Hosmer Morse Foundation, Inc.*

nisierte, die mit ihren verschiedenen Talenten alle zum Gesamterfolg des Unternehmens beitrugen.

Der Mensch, der Traum und die Legende

Unermüdliche, pausenlose Arbeit bringt das Meisterwerk hervor.
Farbe ist für das Auge wie Musik für das Ohr. (L. C. T.)

Für seine Zeitgenossen war Tiffany ein Exzentriker, Autokrat und Perfektionist. Er war ein anspruchsvoller, zugleich aber auch freundlicher und großzügiger Chef, der immer ein offenes Ohr für die Probleme seiner vielen Angestellten hatte. Das Personal in Laurelton Hall fürchtete und verehrte ihn ebenso wie die Beschäftigten in seinen Werkstätten, in denen er oft mit seinem Spazierstock erschien und jedes Stück zerschlug, das seinen Ansprüchen nicht genügte. Es heißt, dass Tiffany ein Stück aus seinem Sortiment nie länger als drei Monate im Laden eines Händlers ließ; war es dann noch nicht verkauft, forderte er es zurück und bot es nur noch per Katalog an. Und wenn ein Posten eines bestimmten Gegenstands nicht innerhalb eines Jahres abgesetzt war, stellte er die Produktion dieses Objekts ein.

Als Privatmann war Tiffany ein treu sorgender Familienvater, der manche Schicksalsschläge hinnehmen musste. Zwei seiner Kinder starben im Säuglingsalter. Seine erste Frau, Mary Woodbridge Goddard, starb 1884 und hinterließ ihm drei Kinder. Seine zweite Frau, Louise Wakeman Knox, eine entfernte Verwandte, starb 1904 und ließ ihn mit drei weiteren Kindern zurück. Als er 1910 erkrankte, wurde er von der aus Irland stammenden Krankenschwester Sarah Handley gesund gepflegt, die bis zu seinem Tod seine Lebensgefährtin blieb. Seinen Heiratsantrag lehnte sie jedoch in Hinblick auf den aus seiner Familie zu erwartenden Widerstand gegen die Eheschließung ab.

Tiffany war ein häuslicher Mensch und nahm nur selten an gesellschaftlichen Veranstaltungen teil. In seinen späten Jahren organisierte er allerdings drei prachtvolle Kostümfeste, zu denen er reiche und prominente Bürger sowie bekannte Politiker und Persönlichkeiten aus der New Yorker Kulturszene einlud. Das erste wurde 1913 in den Ausstellungsräumen an der Madison Avenue veranstaltet, die für dieses »ägyptische Fest« zu einer Stadt an den Ufern des Nils umgestaltet worden waren. Die Gäste wur-

lampes, vases et mosaïques Tiffany. On dit que les aménagements paysagers, à eux-seuls, auraient coûté à l'époque plus d'un million de dollars.

Au cours des années, Tiffany change à plusieurs reprises le nom de sa société. En 1885, elle s'appelle la Tiffany Glass Company, puis en 1892, en concurrence avec la nouvelle usine Corona, elle devient la Tiffany Glass and Decorating Co. Vers 1893, le département verre se scinde en Stourbridge Glass Co. d'une part et Allied Arts Co., d'autre part. En 1900, Allied Arts Co. prend le nom d'Ateliers Tiffany. Les hauts fourneaux Tiffany s'ajoutent au consortium en 1902, pour la production de verre Favrile en grandes quantités. A partir de 1919, Tiffany se retire progressivement de la production au quotidien, mais garde un contrôle personnel sur les chaînes de production. A cette même époque, la division non-verre est réorganisée, elle devient le Tiffany Ecclesiastical Department, qui continue de produire sous la marque Ateliers Tiffany. En 1924, les hauts-fourneaux sont abandonnés et en 1932, les Ateliers Tiffany se déclarent officiellement en faillite, même si d'importantes commandes en attente sont achevées par un groupe d'anciens artisans Tiffany qui prend le nom d'Ateliers Westminster Memorial. Ces changements d'appellation témoignent du fait que, chez Tiffany, la production est organisée en « cellules », et que chaque équipe de dessinateurs et de fabricants est reconnue et appréciée pour ce qu'elle sait apporter à l'ensemble de l'entreprise.

L'homme, le rêve et la légende

Seul un travail permanent, infini, fait le chef-d'œuvre.
La couleur est à l'œil ce que la musique est à l'oreille. (L. C. T.)

D'après ceux qui l'ont bien connu, Tiffany était un excentrique autoritaire et perfectionniste. Il était extrêmement exigeant à l'égard de ses collaborateurs, et pourtant il était aussi bon et généreux avec ses employés, et s'intéressait à leurs problèmes personnels. A Laurelton Hall, le personnel lui accordait un grand respect, mais non sans une certaine crainte. De même pour ses artisans, aux Ateliers, où il avait pour habitude de descendre les allées, cane en main et de briser toute pièce qu'il jugeait inacceptable. On raconte qu'il ne laissait jamais un article attendre sur les étagères plus de trois mois. Après quoi, il le mettait en

children before her death in 1904. During a short illness in 1910 he was nursed to health by Irish-born Sarah Handley, who remained his beloved companion for the rest of his life. Although he greatly desired it, they never married. Tiffany seldom participated in the New York social scene, preferring to spend his time at home. Nonetheless, late in life he began to consolidate his legacy, and in 1913 he organized the first of three lavish parties to which he invited wealthy and prominent citizens, cultural figures, artists and politicians. The pageant was held at Tiffany Studios, which was transformed for the occasion into an Egyptian town on the banks of the Nile. Guests were asked to dress in the style of Cleopatra's time, and even the invitation was printed in hieroglyphs on papyrus scrolls. A year later Tiffany held another dinner party, this time at Laurelton Hall, where his children dressed in Grecian costumes and helped serve the dinner of roasted peacock. The last of the three festivities, a breakfast party and retrospective exhibition of some highlights of his prodigious output, was held at Tiffany Studios to celebrate his 68th birthday. At this event, 45 of his artisans performed a dramatization of the history of art entitled "Quest of Beauty."

In 1918, Tiffany created the Louis Comfort Tiffany Foundation, giving it a substantial cash endowment as well as Laurelton Hall and some of the property surrounding it. It was designed as a summer colony for young artists. Tiffany explained: "It is my dearest wish to help young artists of our country to appreciate more the study of nature, and to assist them in establishing themselves in the Art World." He was closely associated with the residents' activities, supervising the offered coursework and making himself available for advice and guidance. The Foundation suffered serious financial setbacks in the stock market crash of 1929, and residencies were discontinued in 1938. By 1946 the Foundation had ceased regular operations and began selling its assets.

Shortly after World War I, the ever-changing wave of artistic tastes as well as the harsh reality of the war turned the tide against Tiffany and his artistic œuvre. Many of his works were removed from their original locations, discarded by their owners, or even vandalized. His creative legacy was brushed aside. Louis Comfort Tiffany's personal fortune (several million dollars at the time of his father's death in 1902) had been depleted as a result of his

den gebeten, in Kostümen aus der Zeit Kleopatras zu erscheinen, und selbst die Einladungen waren stilgerecht auf Papyrusrollen gedruckt. Im Jahr darauf gab er in Laurelton Hall eine Dinnerparty, auf der seine in griechischen Kostümen gekleideten Kinder den Gästen gebratene Pfauen servierten. Und zu seinem 68. Geburtstag gab er 1916 in den Ausstellungsräumen an der Madison Avenue, in denen zu diesem Anlass eine Retrospektive mit den Höhepunkten seines umfangreichen Schaffens gezeigt wurde, ein Champagner-Frühstück, auf dem 45 seiner Mitarbeiter unter dem Motto »Die Suche nach Schönheit« (»The Quest of Beauty«) eine dramatisierte Darstellung der Geschichte der Kunst aufführten.

1918 gründete Tiffany die Louis Comfort Tiffany Foundation, um begabte junge Künstler zu unterstützen: »Es ist mein liebster Wunsch, dazu beizutragen, jungen Künstlern unseres Landes das Studium der Natur ans Herz zu legen und ihnen dabei zu helfen, sich in der Kunstwelt zu etablieren.« Er stattete diese Stiftung mit beträchtlichen Mitteln aus und stellte ihr Laurelton Hall als Sommerkolonie für junge Künstler zur Verfügung. Er selbst führte die Aufsicht über das Kursangebot und stand den jungen Künstlern als Ratgeber zur Verfügung. 1929 musste die Stiftung einen finanziellen Rückschlag hinnehmen, und 1938 wurde das Wohnheim geschlossen. 1946 stellte die Stiftung ihre Tätigkeiten ein, und das Stiftungsvermögen wurde aufgelöst.

Mit dem Ende des Ersten Weltkriegs begann Tiffanys Stern zu sinken. Die grausame Realität des Krieges hatte einen neuen Zeitgeist hervorgebracht, der seine Ideen und Kreationen als überholt erscheinen ließ. Viele seiner Werke wurden beseitigt oder sogar zerstört. Tiffany geriet in Vergessenheit. Sein extravaganter Lebensstil und seine Stiftung hatten sein Vermögen, das 1902, nach dem Tod seines Vaters, mehrere Millionen Dollar betrug, aufgezehrt. 1932 mussten die Tiffany-Studios Konkurs anmelden. Das Inventar bestand aus 200–300 t Glas in »5000 Farben und Farbtönen«, hauptsächlich in Form ovaler, etwa drei Fuß (ungefähr einen Meter) langer Scheiben. In ungefähr 500 großen Kisten wurden die wertvollen Gläser zunächst einem Geschäftspartner und später einem Anwalt überlassen. Nachdem mehrere Jahrzehnte vergangen waren, wurden die 36 000 Glasplatten von Egon Neustadt für sein geplantes Tiffany-Museum erworben.

A signed photograph of Tiffany in later years.

Signierte Porträtfotografie Tiffanys im vorgerückten Alter.

Photographie signée de Tiffany à l'âge mûr.

Christie's Images.

Leaf and vine centerpiece with flower insert.

Tafelaufsatz mit Weinlaubdekor und herausnehmbarem Blumeneinsatz.

Milieu de table feuille et vigne avec garniture en forme de fleur.

c. 1910. Courtesy Macklowe Gallery, NY.

réserve et le vendait sur catalogue uniquement. Et, si le stock ne se vendait pas dans l'année qui suivait, il mettait fin à la fabrication de l'article en question.

Dans sa vie personnelle, Tiffany a dû faire face à un certain nombre de tragédies. Deux de ses enfants meurent en bas âge. Sa première femme, Mary Woodbridge Godard meurt en 1884, le laissant avec trois enfants. Plus tard, il épouse une cousine éloignée, Louise Wakeman Knox dont il a trois autres enfants, avant qu'elle ne disparaisse à son tour en 1904. Au cours d'une brève maladie, en 1910, il re couvre la santé grâce aux bons soins d'une infirmière d'ori gine irlandaise, Sarah Handley, qui va rester sa compagn jusqu'à la fin de ses jours. Bien qu'il le souhaite ardem ment, jamais ils ne se marieront, Sarah étant trop sen sible à l'opposition de la famille du grand homme.

La plupart du temps, Tiffany préfère rester chez lui et il ne participe qu'exceptionnellement au théâtre de la vie mondaine new-yorkaise. Cependant, à un âge avancé, il commence à consolider son héritage. En 1913, il organise la première de trois fastueuses réceptions ; y sont invités les personnages les plus riches et les plus en vue, les célé brités du monde de la culture, des artistes et des politi ciens. La soirée a lieu aux Ateliers Tiffany, transformés pour l'occasion, en une ville égyptienne des bords du Nil. Les invités sont priés de se costumer dans le style de Cléo pâtre et même les invitations sont imprimées en hiéro glyphes, sur rouleaux de papyrus. L'année suivante, Tiffa ny donne un autre dîner somptueux, cette fois à Laurelton Hall, où ses enfants, en costume grec, servent du paon rôti. La dernière des trois fêtes se tient en 1916, aux Ateliers Tiffany, pour célébrer son 68ème anniversaire. Elle s'organise autour d'un petit-déjeuner et d'une exposition rétrospective présentant quelques pièces maîtresses de son extraordinaire production. A cette occasion, 45 de ses arti sans mettent en scène une représentation de l'histoire de l'art qu'ils intitulent : « La quête de la beauté ».

En 1918, Tiffany crée la Fondation Louis Comfort Tif fany, qu'il dote d'une importante donation financière ainsi que de Laurelton Hall et des terres avoisinantes. Son inten tion est d'en faire une résidence d'été pour jeunes artistes. Tiffany explique : « Mon vœu le plus cher est d'aider ces jeunes Américains à s'attacher davantage à l'étude de la nature et de leur permettre de faire leur chemin dans le monde de l'art. » Il gardera un intérêt constant pour le

extravagant lifestyle and the establishment of the Tiffany Foundation. Tiffany Studios declared bankruptcy in 1932, with an inventory of some 200 to 300 tons of glass constituting a palette of "five thousand colors and hues," primarily in the form of ovals about one meter long. Five hundred large crates containing the precious glass were left to an associate, and later to a lawyer. Several decades later the 36,000 sheets of glass were acquired by Dr. Egon Neustadt, who intended to build a Tiffany museum but died before this dream could be realized.

Louis Comfort Tiffany died in relative obscurity on January 17, 1933 in New York, his spectacular works in glass all but forgotten. In 1938 his New York City residence was demolished, and in the same year over 1,000 items remaining from the stock of Tiffany Studios were auctioned off. It was only in the late 1950's, as pioneers of modern design were being rediscovered, that interest in Tiffany's work was renewed. In 1964 Robert Koch's book *Louis C. Tiffany, Rebel in Glass* was published, and the Art Nouveau movement enjoyed a surge of popularity as a result. Today the interest in Tiffany's creations and aesthetic is at an all-time high. Louis Comfort Tiffany's life was devoted to his "quest of beauty," and his quest was gloriously successful: No American artist before or since has enjoyed such a universal reputation for versatility, creative genius and uniqueness of vision. The name Tiffany is once again associated with luxury, beauty, color and glamour as it was 100 years ago, and more than ever before, is regarded as an integral part of Art Nouveau.

Louis Comfort Tiffany starb am 17. Januar 1933 in New York. 1938 wurde sein Wohnsitz in New York City abgerissen, und im selben Jahr wurden 1000 Objekte aus dem Lager der Tiffany-Studios versteigert. Erst als man in den 1950er-Jahren die Pioniere des modernen Designs wieder entdeckte, wurde auch das Interesse an seinem Werk erneut geweckt. 1964 veröffentlichte Robert Koch sein Buch »Louis C. Tiffany, Rebel in Glass« und löste damit eine neue Welle der Begeisterung für den Jugendstil aus. Heute ist das Interesse an Tiffanys Kreationen und seiner Ästhetik größer als je zuvor. Wie vor 100 Jahren wird sein Name wieder mit Luxus, Schönheit, Farbe und Glamour assoziiert, und sein Werk wird mehr denn je als beispielhaft für den Jugendstil betrachtet. Sein ganzes Leben war der »Suche nach Schönheit« gewidmet, und diese Suche war von Erfolg gekrönt: Er hat mit seinen Kreationen große Kunst hervorgebracht, und mit seiner beispiellosen Kreativität, Virtuosität und Vielseitigkeit hat Louis Comfort Tiffany eine weltweite Popularität gewonnen, die von keinem anderen amerikanischen Künstler so leicht übertroffen werden dürfte.

Mosaic box with dragonfly motif.
Mosaikkästchen mit Libellendekor.
Boîte en mosaïque au motif de libellule.
c. 1908.
Courtesy Macklowe Gallery, NY.

activités de ses résidents, supervisant les cours qui leur sont donnés et restant lui-même disponible pour prodiguer conseils et avis. La Fondation subit un sérieux revers financier en 1929, et les séjours sont supprimés en 1938. A partir de 1946, la Fondation cesse toute activité régulière et commence à vendre son patrimoine.

Peu après la fin de la Première Guerre mondiale, l'évolution inévitable des goûts artistiques, ainsi que les dures réalités de la guerre, se retournent contre Tiffany et son œuvre. Nombre de ses réalisations sont retirées de leur emplacement d'origine, mises au rebut par leur propriétaire ou même vandalisées. L'apport créatif de Tiffany est sous la forme d'ovales d'environ un mètre de long. Cinq cents énormes caisses contenant ce verre précieux sont remises à l'un des associés, puis à un avocat. Quelques dizaines d'années après, les 36 000 plaques de verre sont achetées par le Dr Egon Neustadt, qui se propose de fonder un musée Tiffany.

Louis Comfort Tiffany meurt dans l'obscurité, le 17 janvier 1933, à New York. Ses extraordinaires verreries sont presque tombées dans l'oubli. En 1938, sa résidence new-yorkaise est démolie. La même année, plus de 1 000 objets du stock des Ateliers sont dispersés aux enchères. Il faudra attendre les années 1950, et la redécouverte des pionniers du design moderne, pour que renaisse l'intérêt pour son œuvre. En 1964, avec la publication de l'ouvrage de Robert Koch, « Louis C. Tiffany, le rebelle du verre », le mouvement Art Nouveau connaît un regain de popularité. Aujourd'hui, l'intérêt pour les créations et l'esthétique de Tiffany bat son plein. Dans sa « Quête de la beauté », longue d'un demi-siècle, Tiffany a su transcender sa recherche de notoriété en grand art. Aucun artiste américain avant lui, et aucun depuis, n'a connu une telle réputation à l'échelle mondiale, pour la multiplicité de ses talents, sa créativité et son point de vue visionnaire. A nouveau, le nom de Tiffany se trouve associé à l'idée de luxe, de beauté, de couleur, de séduction, et plus que jamais, il demeure partie essentielle de l'Art Nouveau.

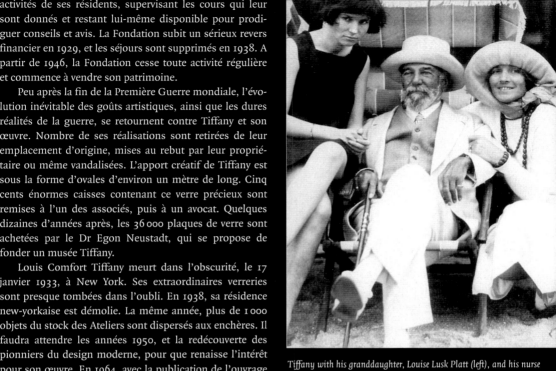

Tiffany with his granddaughter, Louise Lusk Platt (left), and his nurse Sarah Handley (right).

Tiffany mit seiner Enkelin Louise Lusk Platt (links) und seiner Pflegerin Sarah Handley (rechts).

Tiffany avec sa petite-fille Louise Lusk Platt (à gauche) et son infirmière Sarah Handley (à droite).

c. 1930. Courtesy Alastair Duncan, NY.

Necklace with black opal pendant.

Halskette mit Anhänger aus schwarzem Opal.

Collier avec un pendant d'opale noir.

Courtesy Macklowe Gallery, NY.

Leaded Glass Windows

Bleiverglasungen

Vitraux au verre au plomb

Landscape window, c. 1925

Eggplants, leaded transom, 1879

Feeding the flamingos, c. 1892

The House of Aldus, 1897

Butterfly window, c. 188-

Parakeets and gold fish bowl, 1893

Rose window, 1906

"THE GREATEST OF THESE IS CHARITY."
IN LOVING MEMORY OF
1830-ANTHONY J. DREXEL-1893
FROM L.L.B.

Memorial window, c. 1898

Aurora (Young woman at fountain), 1894

Au Nouveau Cirque, Papa Chrys

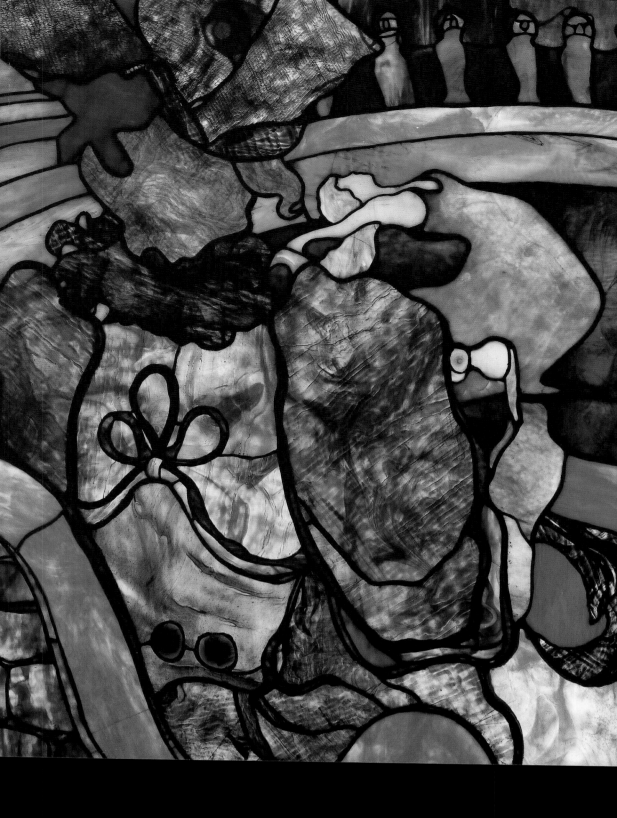

SPRING

Summer

Autumn

A TOKEN·OF·THE·LOVE·SARAH·GIBBS·THOMPSON
BEARS·TO·THESE·LITTLE·CHILDREN

Sarah Gibbs Thompson memorial window, c. 1890

Three panel leaded glass screen, c. 1900

NOW HIRAM THE KING OF TYRE HAD FURNISHED
SOLOMON WITH CEDAR TREES, AND FIR TREES, AND
WITH GOLD, ACCORDING TO ALL HIS DESIRE. I KINGS, IXXI
A LOVING TRIBUTE TO
M. W. TOWNSEND SCUDDER
PAST GRAND MASTER OF MASONS IN THE STATE OF
NEW YORK & TRUSTEE OF THE MASONIC HOME AT UTICA
1906 PRESENTED BY HIS OFFICIAL STAFF 1908

M.W. Townsend Scudder memorial window, c. 1908

Barrett memorial window, c. 1900

An angel in profile, c. 1904

ial window, c. 1905

The sacrifice, c. 1905

The boy Jesus preaching in the temple, c. 1906

Class of 1902 memorial window, c. 1905

"VNTIL THE DAY BREAK, AND
THE SHADOWS FLEE AWAY"

✠ ✠ CLASS OF ✠ ✠
NINETEEN HVNDRED AND TWO

Kempner memorial window, 1888

Landscape window, 1905

AND WITH THE MORN
THOSE ANGEL FACES
SMILE WHICH WE HAVE

LOVED LONG SINCE
AND LOST AWHILE

The story of the cross, c. 1892

IN LOVING MEMORY OF MY DEAR PARENTS
ELLIS AND BARBETTE MITTELDORFER
BY THEIR DAUGHTER

Volcano, Beth-El Synagogue, Richmond, VA, 1923   Leaded glass window with flowering
magnolia trees and irises, c. 1920

Triptych for the Red Cross Headquarters, Washington, DC, 1917

Landscape with birch
tree and irises, c. 1917

Lake landscape
with irises, c. 1915

The 10 commandments, Temple Emmanu-el, New York, c. 1925

113

Square landscape, 1916

Autumn landscape

Angel of peace, c. 1904

Bradbury memorial window, c. 1880–1890

King David playing the harp, c. 1905

Landscape window,
c. 1900–1920

Woman greeting the sun, c. 1895

Landscape with iris and flowering magnolia, c. 1905

Bigelow memorial landscape window, c. 1907

Landscape window

Landscape window, c. 1910

Landscape with flowering fruit trees, 1913

Landscape with flowering fruit trees (detail), 1913

Winifield memorial window, c. 1890

Peacock leaded glass window, c. 1910

Lamps
Lampen
Lampes

Table lamp with drophead blue-eyed dragonflies (detail), c. 1910

Previous page: Geometric leaded and Favrile glass and bronze table lamp (detail), c. 1910

12-light lily lamp, 1900–1910

Pair of 3-light lily desk lamps, c. 1905–1908

7-light lily table lamp with bronze lilypad base, c. 1905

Spider table lamp, c. 1900–1910

Magnolia floor lamp,
c. 1903

Magnolia floor lamp (detail), c. 1903

146

Lotus bell lamp, c. 1905

Mandarin table

149

Poppy filigree floor lamp,
c. 1899–1920

Poppy table lamp, undated

Spreading cherry table lamp,
c. 1899–1920

Elaborate grape table lamp, c. 1900-1905

Flowering lotus table lamp, c. 1903

Pair of desk lamps, c. 1910

Pineapple table lamp, c. 1905–1910

Reading lamp, c. 1900

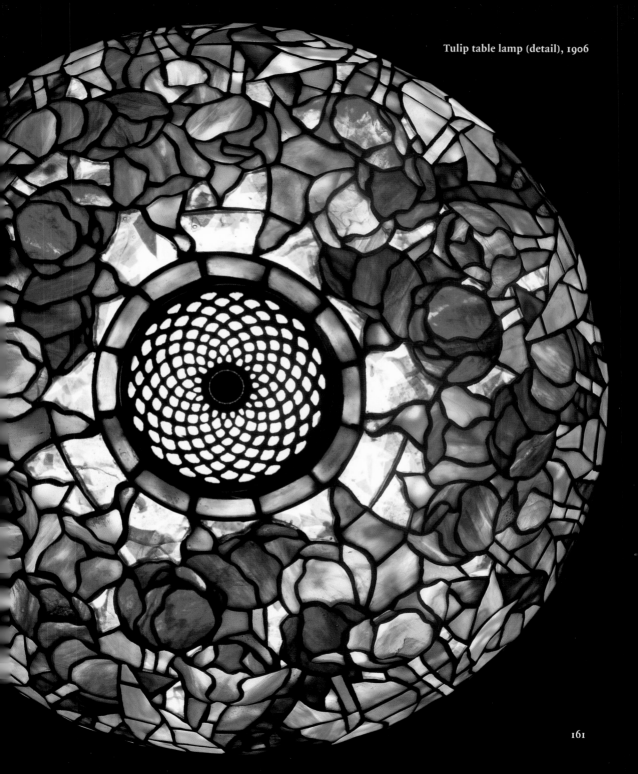

Tyler table lamp, c. 1905–1907

Acorn table lamp, c. 1910

Swirling leaf table lamp, c. 1905

Greek key table lamp, c. 1907

One-of-a-kind peacock
centerpiece table lamp, c. 1898
Opposite left: details of
shade and base

Peacock table lamp (detail), c. 1900

Peacock table lamp, c. 1905

Geometric table lamp, undated

Dogwood table lamp, c. 1905

Belted dogwood table lamp, c. 1905

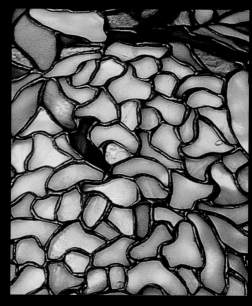

Laburnum floor lamp (detail), 1903

Laburnum floor lamp, 1903

**Peony table lamp,
c. 1905–1908**

**Elaborate peony table
lamp, c. 1901**

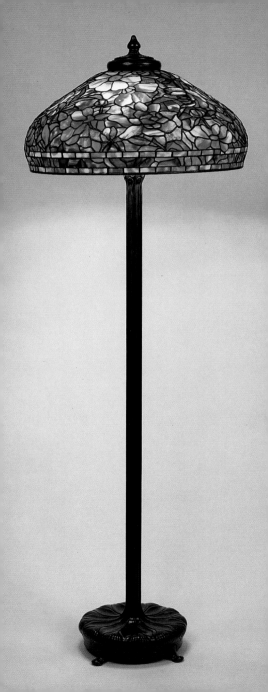

Lily pad table lamp, c. 1905–1910

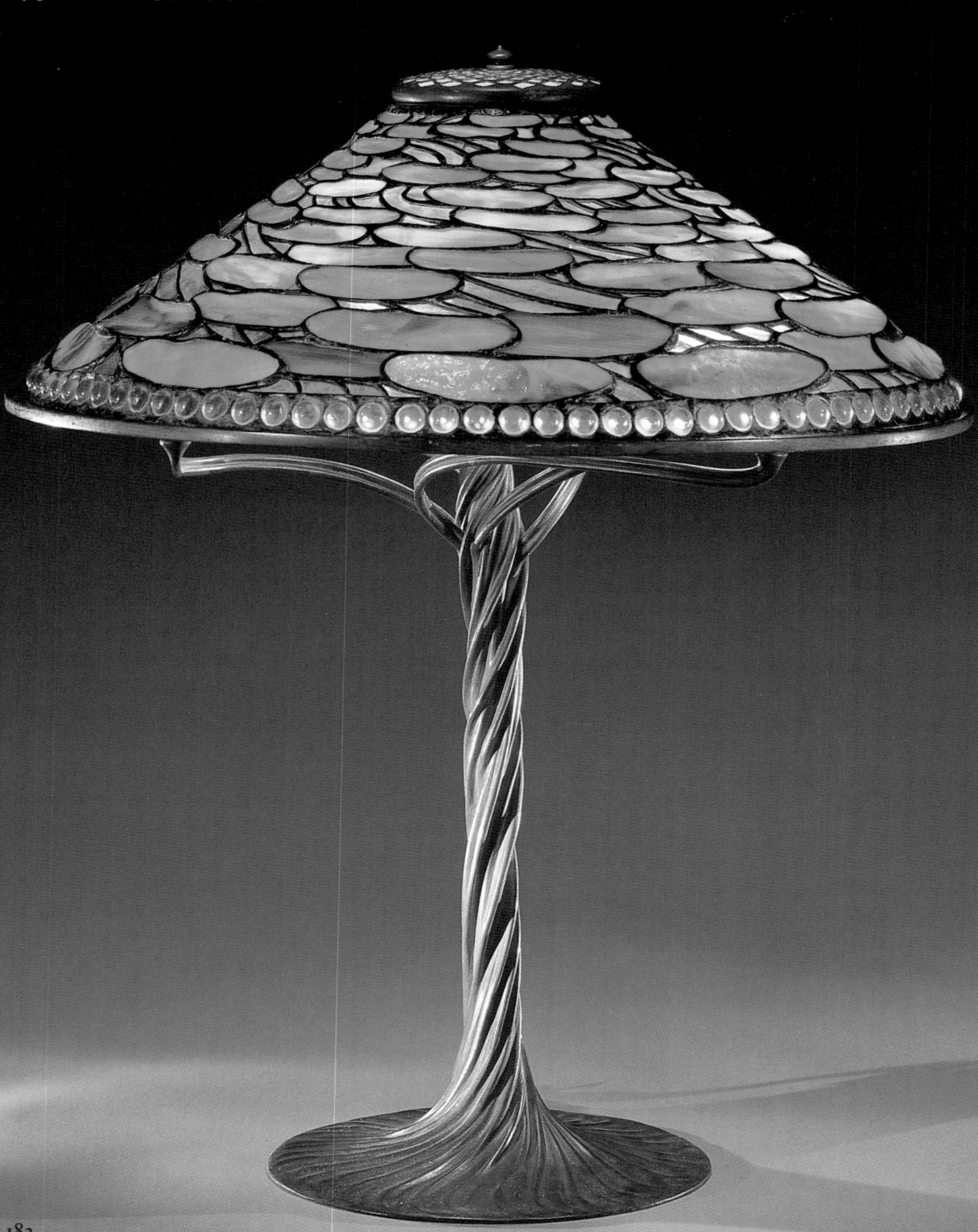

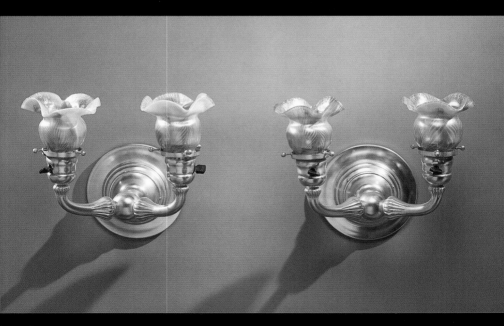

Pair of sconces, c. 1910

Peony border floor
lamp, c. 1910

Peony border floor lamp
(detail), c. 1910

Filigree Moorish table lamp, c. 1895

Green lotus lamp, c. 1900–1910

Pink lotus lamp, c. 1900–1910

Red lotus lamp, 1900–1910

Tulip table lamp, c. 1905

Wild rose border table lamp, c. 1910–1915

Cyclamen table lamp, c. 1903

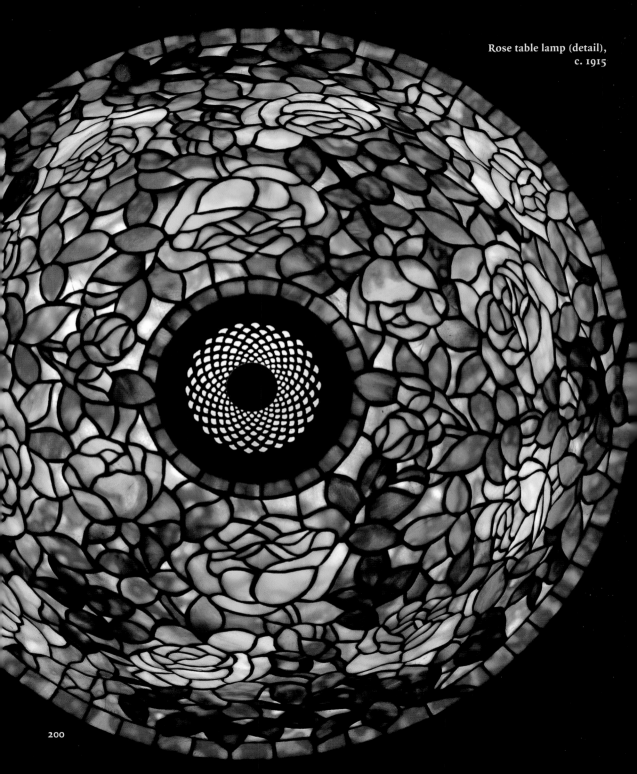

Rose table lamp, c.1915

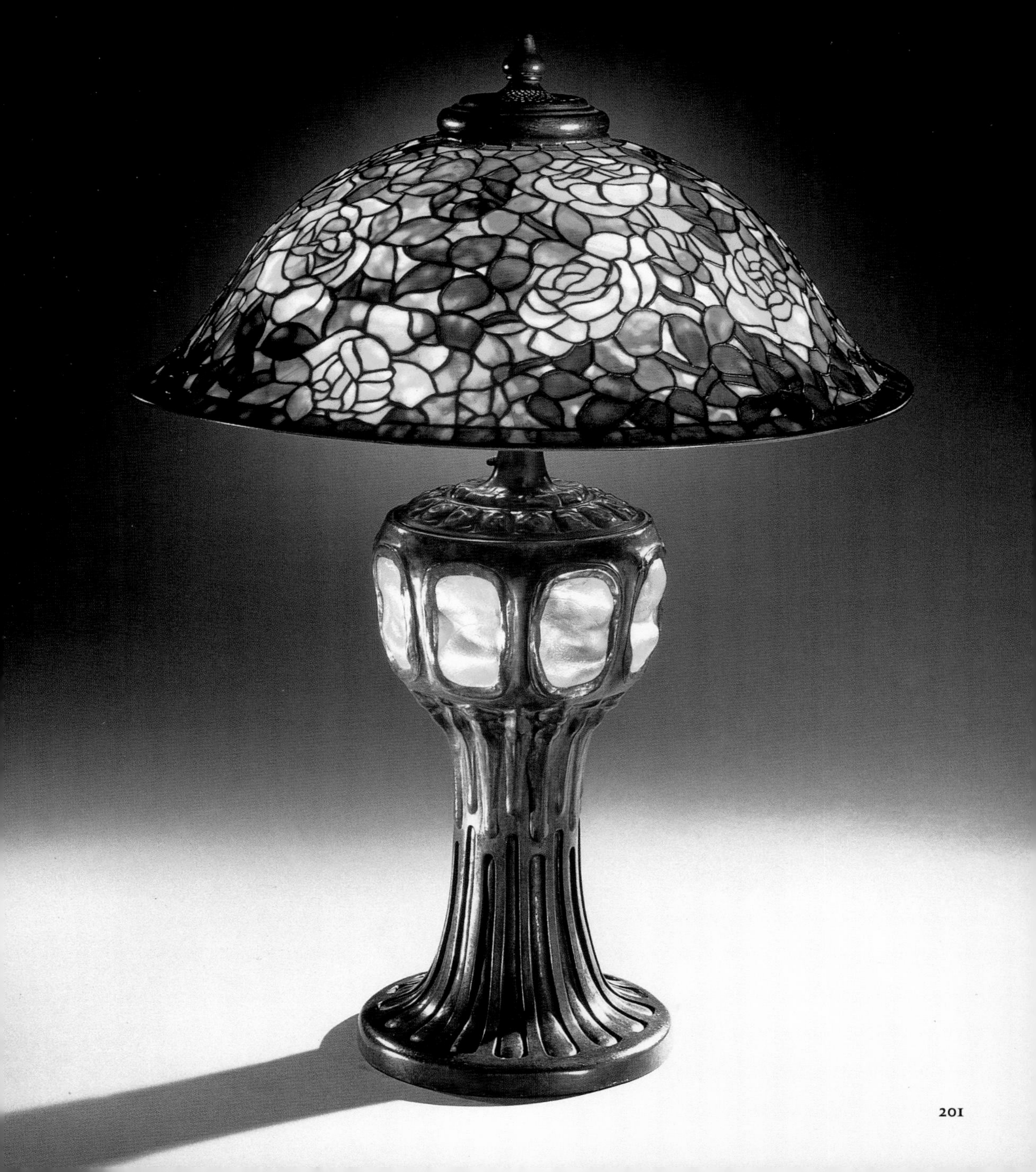

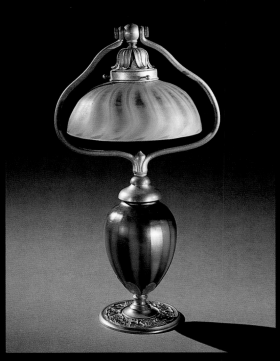

Desk lamp, c. 1904

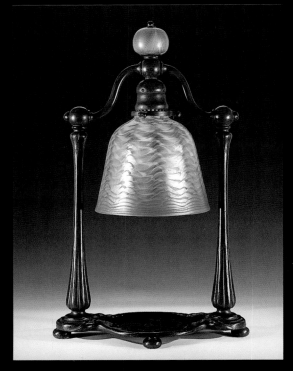

Bell table lamp, c. 1902

Desk lamp, c. 1900

Peony table lamp (detail), c. 1902

Peony table lamp, c. 1902

Tulip table lamp, c. 1905–1908

Daffodil with dogwood
border table lamp, c. 1905–1908

Daffodil table lamp, c. 1901

Daffodil and narcissus tabl

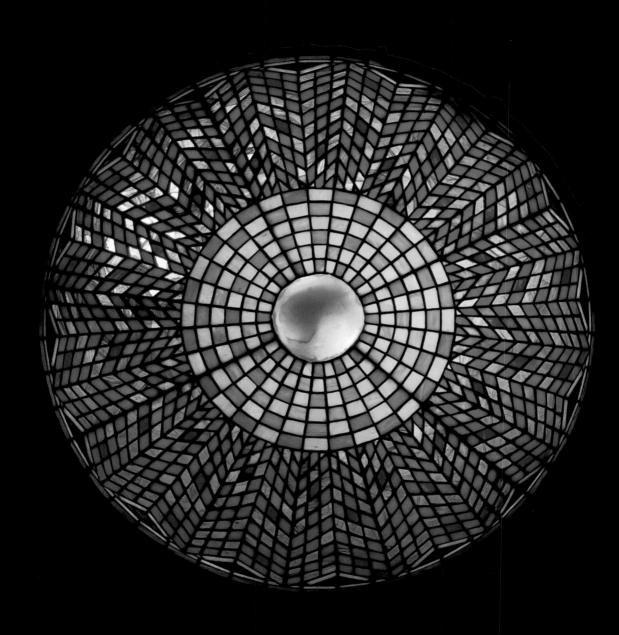

Aztec geometric lampshade, c. 1910

Geometric table lamp
with balls, c. 1910

Geometric table lamp,
c. 1900–1908

Greek key
table lamp,
c. 1902

Herringbone
table lamp,
c. 1910

Pomegranate table lamp, c. 1910

Mushroom table lamp, c. 1898

Acorn table lamp, c. 1910

Kerosene table lamp, c. 1898

221

Dragonfly table lamp, c. 1900

Bell flower table lamp, c. 1915

Woodbine foliage table lamp, c. 1915

Three Favrile glass and bronze candlestick lamps, c. 1910–1917

Damascene table lamp, c. 1900

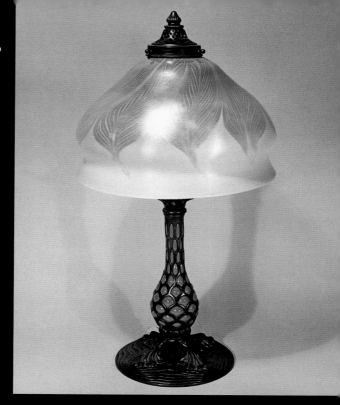

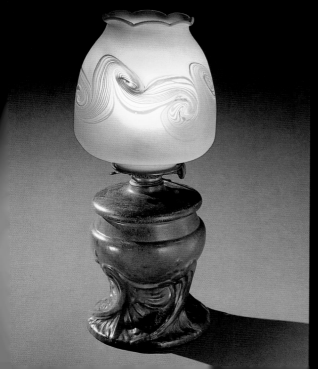

Glass and ceramic table lamp, c. 1898

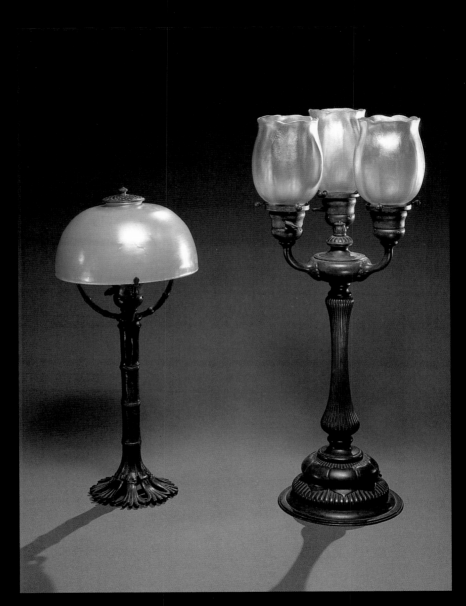

Two desk lamps, c. 1905

Candlestick lamp, c. 1902

229

Nasturtium on trellis hanging lamp, 1903

Autumn leaves chandelier, c. 1903

Rare trumpet creeper hanging lamp, c. 1903

Trumpet creeper table lamp, c. 1899–1910

237

Moorish-style chandelier,
c. 1899–1920

228

Dragonfly hanging lamp, 1899–1920

Dogwood cone-shaped hanging lamp, c. 1904

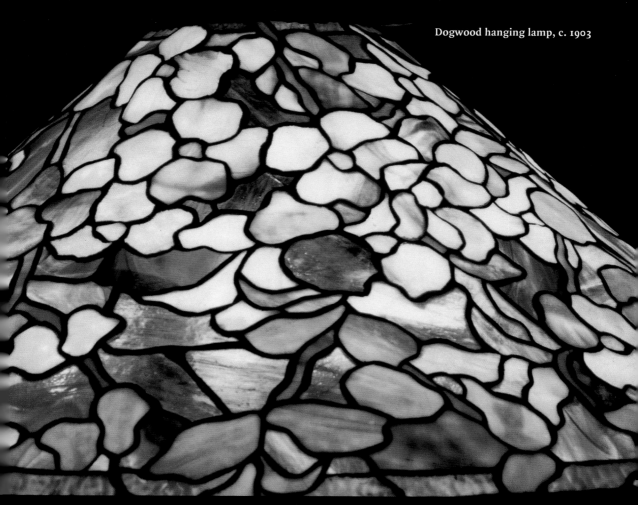

Dogwood hanging lamp, c. 1903

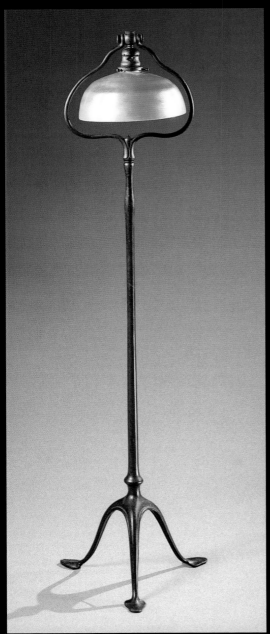

Harp-arm tripod floor lamp, 1910–1915

Linen-fold floor lamp, c. 1915–1920

244

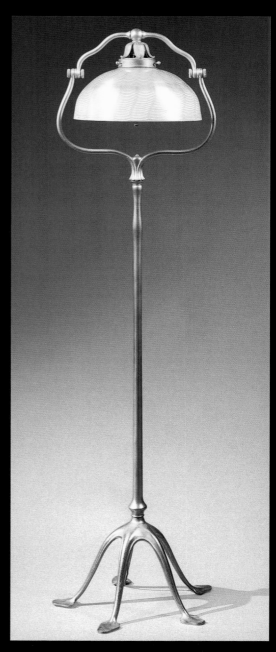

Harp-arm floor lamp, c. 1910–1915

Harp-arm damascene floor lamp, c. 1910–1915

Magnolia floor lamp,
c. 1905

Magnolia floor lamp
(detail), c. 1905

246

Lotus chandelier, undated

Lotus chandelier (detail), undated

Vases
Vasen

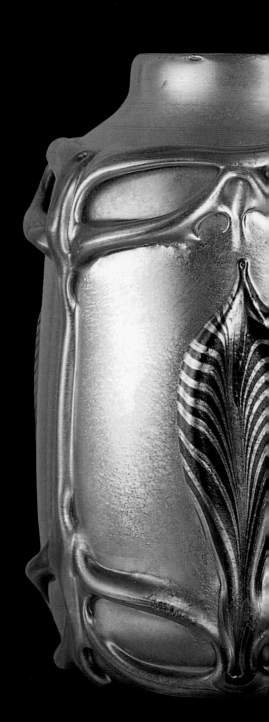

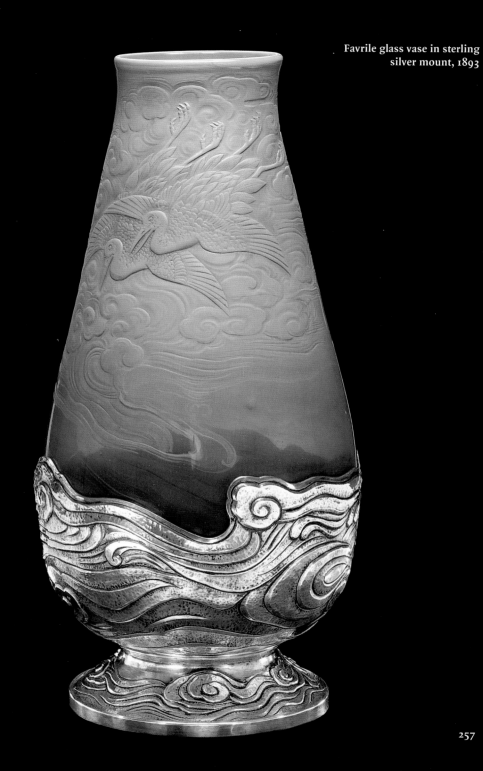

Favrile glass vase with silver mount and inlay, c. 1896

Peacock eye (left), flower form (center),
Favrile glass with hearts and vine (right), c. 1900–1905

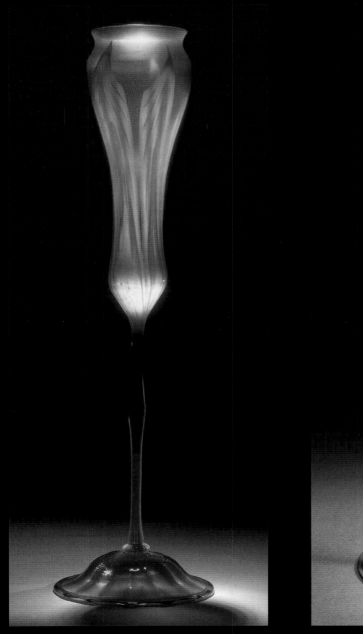

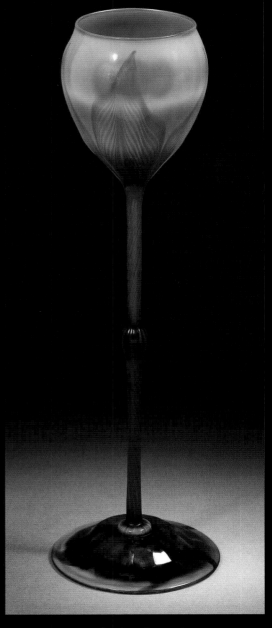

Favrile glass flower-form vase, c. 1903

Favrile glass flower-form vase, c. 1900

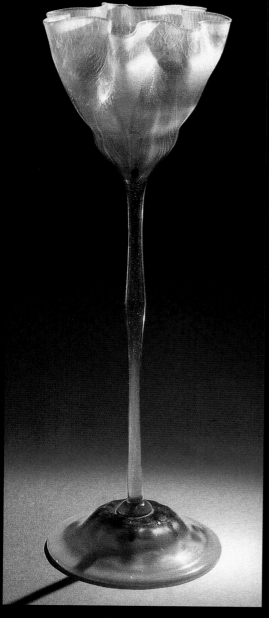

Favrile glass flower-form vase, c. 1900

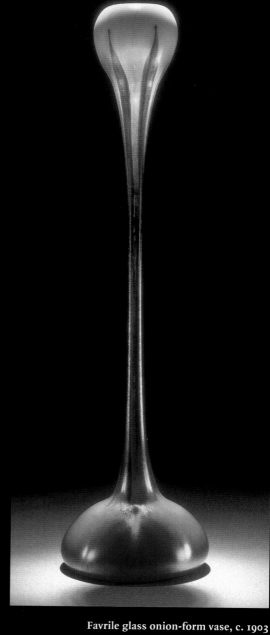

Favrile glass onion-form vase, c. 1903

263

$ 10 to 20

40 & 60?

Flint glass continued

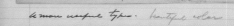

Good Threads

from 50 to 100 or so

A more useful types. beautiful color

'5'

The passing year brought more refinement
of form & made more money, but skated it

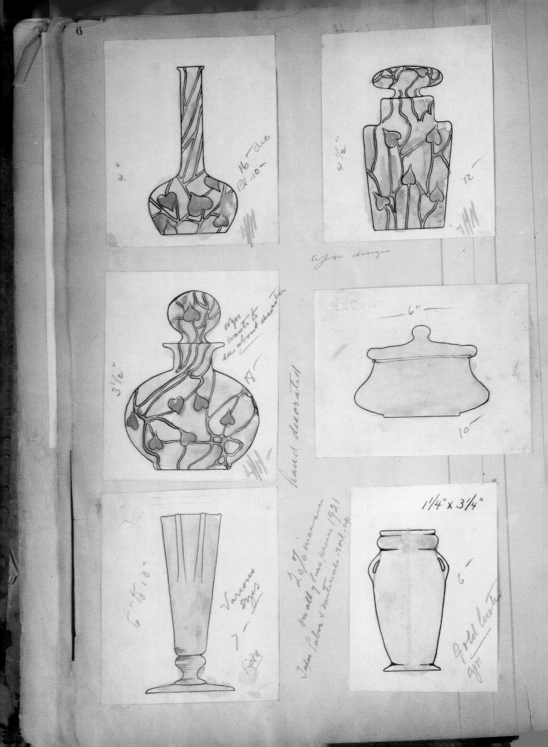

6

4"

16 — duo
Pt -10-

4½"

12

3½"

aga wants to
see about decoration

8"

ayn drayer

Panel decorated

6"

10

6" 8 10

Varinus
types

7
Roby

20% increase
Parall glass Porino 1921
Vifer Color & Material rd. up.

1¼" x 3¼"

6"

Gold luster
ayn

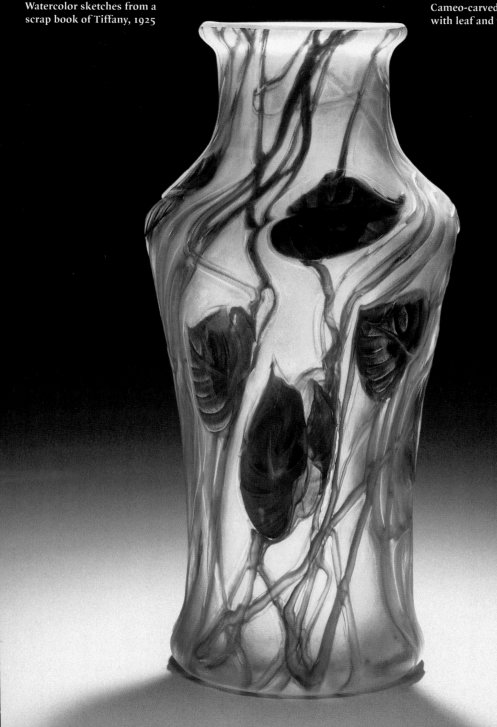

Three vases and a bowl,
all of Favrile glass, c. 1900–1905

Opposite left: Persian peacock-eye rosewater sprinkler, c. 1905
Opposite right: Favrile glass peacock vase, 1905

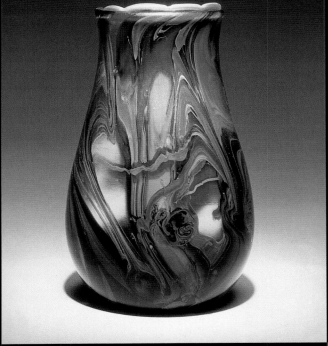

Three flower-form Favrile glass vases, c. 1896–1900

Leaf-and-vine vase, c. 1905

Paperweight vase with gold inserts, c. 1903

Production of a Favrile glass vase at the Tiffany Studios

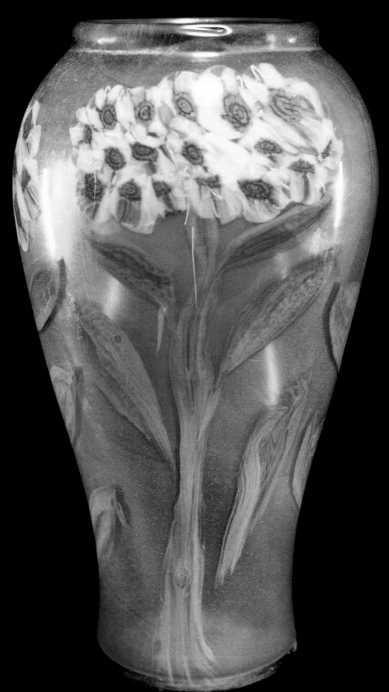

Three vases, c. 1905–1908

Cypriot vase, c. 1910

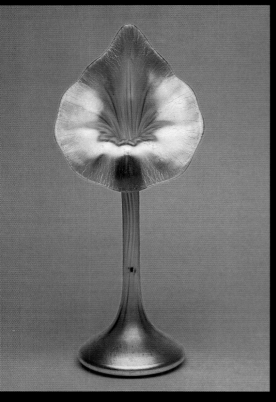

Jack-in-the-pulpit vase, c. 1900

Jack-in-the-pulpit vase, c. 1900

Group of vases, c. 1898–1905

Rare midnight blue vase, c. 1898

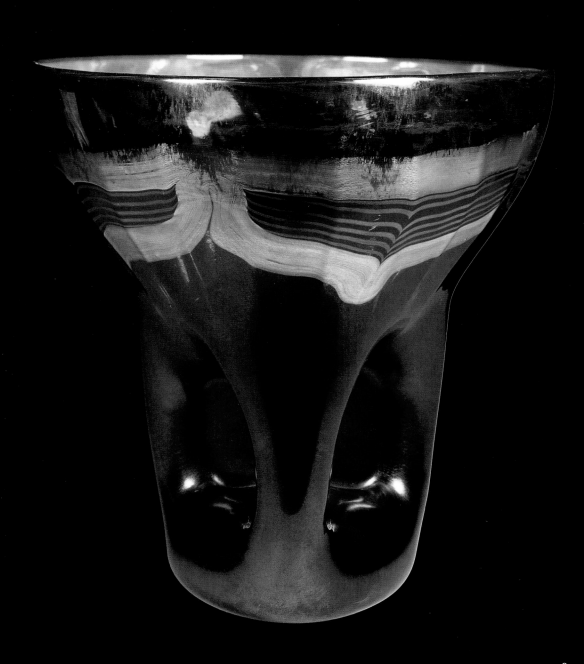

285

Paperweight glass vase, c. 1904

Lava vase, c. 1907

Cameo glass vase, c. 1905

287

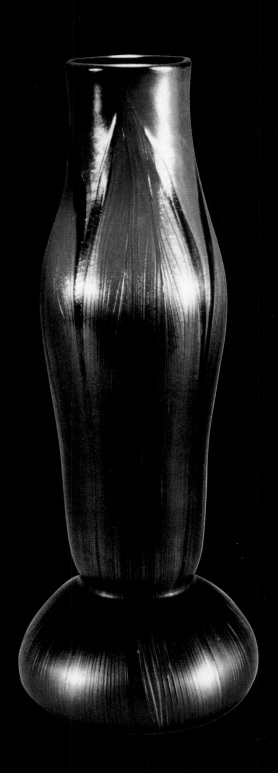

Paperweight glass vase, c. 1906

Paperweight glass vase, c. 1904

Onion-form vase, c. 1906

289

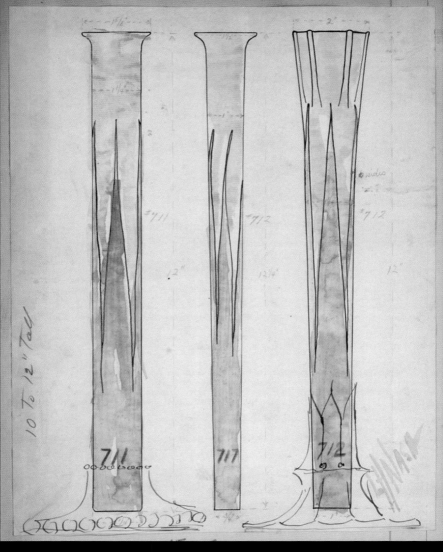

Watercolor sketches from a scrap book of Tiffany, 1925

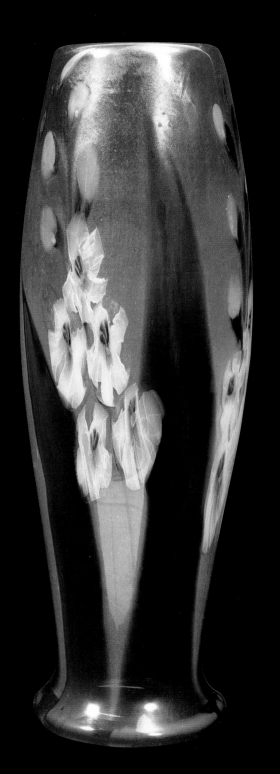

Paperweight vase
with flowers, c. 1905

Blue vase, c. 1904

Early Tiffany Favrile Glass
1893-4 to about 1918

20"   14"   lamp globe   8"

All prices of Favrile Glass - were established
not on production records but on
artistic merit - alone.

The numbers on the small tags
do not tell the age of the piece - they are
applied only when shipment is made.

numbering started from #1 to 10000
then A1 - A2 up to A10000 then B1 - B2 est
to A10000 and so on - then 1A - 2A est to 10000

31

Iridescence was not much used at this time
but later the public demanded it.

18"   25"   20"   10"   15"

All glass was marked

L C T   L.C. Tiffany   L.C. Tiffany Favrile

Favrile — Ex Louis C. Tiffany or Exhibition
sometimes the place — as Paris Ex Louis C Tiffany Favrile
all of the above bore a number —
        with the exception of table glass ware,
such as wine glasses and small articles
large fruit bowls will have a number
also comports — will bore a letter which
represents a certain decoration —
Small lighting glass — globes cut (Favrile)

L H Nash
Designer + Production mgr.

Two lava vases, c. 1910

Group of ceramic objects,
vases and lamp bases,
c. 1905

Catalogue
Katalog

Wall mosaic in the Curtis Center, Philadelphia
Photograph, ©Jeffrey Totaro, Bryn Mawr, PA

68   69   70   71

Lake landscape beneath a multi-
colored cloudy sky (detail of
p. 107).
Seenlandschaft unter farbenreicher
Wolkenformation (Detail von
S. 107).
Vitrail représentant les grèves d'un
lac sous un ciel de nuages multicolores (détail de la p. 107).
134 x 82.5 cm.
c. 1915.
Christie's Images.

Trumpet vine window, Tiffany
Studios.
Klettertrompeten-Fenster der
Tiffany Studios.
Vitrail au motif de vigne, Tiffany
Studios.
91.4 x 86.4 cm.
c. 1910.
Courtesy Marchese & Co., Santa
Barbara, CA.

Landscape window.
Fenster mit Landschaftsmalerei.
Vitrail représentant un paysage.
81.3 x 68.6 cm.
c. 1925.
Courtesy Marchese & Co., Santa
Barbara, CA.

72   73   74   75

Eggplants, leaded transom.
Bleiverglastes Oberlicht mit
Auberginenmotiv.
Vitrail en verre au plomb au motif
d'aubergines.
81.3 x 106.7 cm.
c. 1879.
Collection of the Charles Hosmer
Morse Museum of American Art,
Winter Park, FL, © The Charles
Hosmer Morse Foundation, Inc.

"Feeding the Flamingos," created
for the 1893 Chicago World's
Columbian Exposition.
»Die Fütterung der Flamingos«,
ausgeführt für die World's Colum-
bian Exposition in Chicago 1893.
« La Nourriture des flamants », créé
pour l'Exposition Colombienne
Internationale en 1893.
h: 157 cm.
c. 1892.
Collection of the Charles Hosmer
Morse Museum of American Art,
Winter Park, FL, © The Charles
Hosmer Morse Foundation, Inc.

Living room at Laurelton Hall.
Wohnzimmer in Laurelton Hall.
Salon à Laurelton Hall.
Season photograph.
Christie's Images.

76

77

78

79

"The House of Aldus, 1897." William Howard Hart memorial window depicting Aldus Manutius in his Venice printing house in 1502.
Das Haus von Aldus, 1897. Buntglasfenster zum Gedenken an William Howard Hart. Es zeigt Aldus Manutius in seinem venezianischen Druckhaus 1502.
La maison d'Aldus, 1897. Vitrail en mémoire de William Howard Hart, montrant Aldus Manutius dans son imprimerie à Venise en 1502.
Courtesy Alastair Duncan, NY.

Butterfly window, created for Tiffany's house at 72th/Madison St., NY.
Schmetterlingsfenster, ausgeführt für das Tiffany-Haus an der 72th/Madison St., NY.
Vitrail au motif de papillon, créé pour la maison de Tiffany à 72th/Madison St., NY.
161.3 x 165.1 cm.
c. 1885.
Collection of the Charles Hosmer Morse Museum of American Art, Winter Park, FL,

Parakeets and gold fish bowl. This important leaded and plated glass window was created for the 1893 World's Columbian Exposition.
Sittiche und Goldfischbecken. Dieses wichtige bleiverglaste und plattierte Fenster wurde für die World's Columbian Exposition in Chicago 1893 hergestellt.
Perroquets avec un bocal à poissons rouges. Cet important Vitrail en verre au plomb plaqué a été créé

pour l'Exposition Colombienne Internationale en 1893.
193.1 x 97.8 cm.
1893.
Christie's Images.

Glass shop at Tiffany Studios.
Glasfensteratelier in den Tiffany Studios.
Atelier de vitraux des Tiffany Studios.
c. 1913. Private collection.

80

81

82

83

Rose window.
Fenster mit Rosendekor.
Vitrail au décor de rose.
175.3 x 144.8 cm.
1906.
Collection of the Charles Hosmer Morse Museum of American Art, Winter Park, FL, © The Charles Hosmer Morse Foundation, Inc.

Memorial window, location unknown.
Gedenkfenster, unbekannter Ort.
Vitrail commémoratif, localisation inconnue.
c. 240 x 180 cm.
c. 1898.
Courtesy Alastair Duncan, NY.

Aurora (Young woman at fountain). Based on a painting by Will Low.
Aurora (Junge Frau am Brunnen). Nach einem Gemälde von Will Low.
L'Aurore (Jeune femme au puits). D'après une peinture de Will Low.
147.3 x 88.9 cm.
1894.
Collection of the Charles Hosmer Morse Museum of American Art, Winter Park, FL, © The Charles Hosmer Morse Foundation, Inc.

"Au Nouveau Cirque, Papa Chrysanthème" after an original work by Toulouse-Lautrec, commissioned by S. Bing.
»Au nouveau cirque, papa chrysanthème«, nach einem Original von Toulouse-Lautrec im Auftrag von S. Bing.
« Au nouveau cirque, papa chrysanthème », d'après un ouvrage original de Toulouse-Lautrec, commissionné par S. Bing.
120 x 85 cm / 1894–1895.
Collection of the Musée d'Orsay, Paris; photo: G. Blot/RMN.

84

85

86

87

Four Seasons windows, created for
the 1900 Exposition Universelle in
Paris.
Vier-Jahreszeiten-Fenster, ausge-
führt für die Pariser Weltausstel-
lung von 1900.
Vitrail des quatre saisons, créé
pour l'Exposition Universelle de
Paris en 1900.
Collection of The Charles Hosmer
Morse Museum of American Art,
Winter Park, FL, © The Charles
Hosmer Morse Foundation, Inc.
Photos: Allan Maxwell.

LEFT / LINKS / A GAUCHE
Spring.
Frühjahr.
Le Printemps.
103.6 x 99.1 cm.
c. 1899–1900.

RIGHT / RECHTS / A DROITE
Summer.
Sommer.
L'Eté.
99.1 x 95.9 cm.
c. 1899–1900.

Four Seasons window series.
Vier-Jahreszeiten-Fenster.
Vitraux des quatre saisons.
Autumn.
Herbst.
L'Automne.
99.1 x 93 cm.
c. 1899–1900.

Winter.
Winter.
L'Hiver.
99.1 x 81.3 cm.
c. 1899–1900.

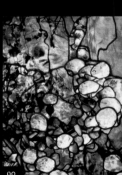

88

89

90

91

Bodine memorial window (Christ
blessing children).
Bodine-Gedenkfenster (Jesus
segnet die Kinder).
Vitrail en mémoire de Bodine
(Jésus bénit les enfants).
First Methodist Episcopal Church,
Germantown, PA.
c. 1895.
Courtesy Alastair Duncan, NY.

Sarah Gibbs Thompson memorial
window (Christ blessing children).
Sarah-Gibbs-Thompson-Gedenk-
fenster (Jesus segnet die Kinder).
Vitrail en mémoire de Sarah Gibbs
Thompson (Jésus bénit les
enfants).
c. 1899.
Courtesy Alastair Duncan, NY.

"Snowball".
An important glass panel made by
Tiffany for the 1900 Exposition
Universelle in Paris.
Ein wichtiger Glasparavent, angefertigt für die Pariser Weltausstellung 1900.
Un paravent de verre important
créé pour l'Exposition Universelle
de Paris en 1900.
80 x 80 cm.

Three-panel leaded glass screen
first shown at the 1900 Paris
Exposition Universelle.
Dreiteiliger bleiverglaster Paravent,
erstmals auf der Weltausstellung
Paris 1900 gezeigt.
Paravent en verre au plomb en trois
parties, présenté pour la première
fois à l'Exposition Universelle de
Paris en 1900.
c. 1900.

92   93   94   95

M. W. Townsend Scudder memorial window (King Solomon, based on 1 Kings 9:11.
M.-W.-Townsend-Scudder-Gedenkfenster mit König Salomon nach 1 Kön 9,11.
Vitrail en mémoire de M. W. Townsend Scudder avec le roi Salomon selon 1 Rois 9,11.
c. 1908.
Courtesy Alastair Duncan, NY.

Barrett memorial window (Christ blessing children).
Barret-Gedenkfenster (Jesus segnet die Kinder).
Vitrail en mémoire de Barret (Jésus bénit les petits enfants).
Christ Episcopal Church, Greenwich, CT.
c. 1900.
Courtesy Alastair Duncan, NY.

Martha Anderson Brown memorial window (Saint Paul preaching at Athens).
Martha-Anderson-Brown-Gedenkfenster (Paulus predigt in Athen).
Vitrail en mémoire de Martha Anderson Brown (St. Paul prêche à Athènes).
St. Paul's Episcopal Church, Rochester, NY.
c. 1905.
Courtesy Alastair Duncan, NY.

Leaded glass window with an angel in profile.
Bleiverglastes Fenster mit einem Engel im Profil.
Vitrail en verre au plomb d'un ange présenté de profil.
74.3 x 54 cm.
c. 1904.
Christie's Images.

96   97   98   99

Memorial window (The sacrifice), location unknown.
Gedenkfenster (Das Opfer). Ort unbekannt.
Vitrail commémoratif (Le sacrifice). Localisation inconnue.
270 x 165 cm.
c. 1905.
Courtesy Alastair Duncan, NY.

The boy Jesus preaching in the Temple.
Jesus predigt als Kind im Tempel.
Le jeune Jésus prêchant au temple.
First Methodist Episcopal Church, Germantown, PA.
c. 1906.
Courtesy Alastair Duncan, NY.

Class of 1902 memorial window.
Gedenkfenster für die Klasse von 1902.
Vitrail commémoratif de la classe de 1902.
c. 1905.
Courtesy Alastair Duncan, NY.

Kempner memorial window (Christ leaving the praetorium).
After a painting by Gustave Doré.
Kempner-Gedenkfenster (Christus verlässt das Praetorium). Nach einem Gemälde von Gustave Doré.
Vitrail en mémoire de Kempner (Jésus-Christ quittant le prétoire). D'après une peinture de Gustave Doré.
St. Paul's Episcopal Church, Milwaukee, WI.
c. 1888.
Courtesy Alastair Duncan, NY.

Landscape window, created for the Beltzhoover home in Irving-on-the-Hudson, NY.
Landschaftsfenster, angefertigt für das Beltzhoover-Haus in Irving-on-the-Hudson, NY.
Vitrail de paysage, créé pour la maison Beltzhoover, à Irving-on-the-Hudson, NY.
364 x 330 cm.
c. 1905.
Collection of The Corning Museum of Glass, Corning, NY.

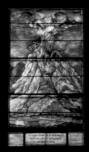

100   101   102   103

Morning glories memorial window. Gedenkfenster mit Windemotiv. Vitrail commémoratif au motif de liseron.
Unitarian Church, Northampton, · MA.
c. 1905.
Courtesy Alastair Duncan, NY.

RIGHT / RECHTS / A DROITE
Circular leaded glass window (Jesus Christ as Pantocrator), probably created for the 1893 Columbian Exposition in Chicago.

Rundfenster (Jesus Christus Pantokrator), wahrscheinlich ausgeführt für die World's Columbian Exposition in Chicago 1893. Fenêtre ronde (Jésus-Christ Pantocrator), probablement créée pour l'Exposition Colombienne Internationale en 1893.
Ø 265.4 cm.
c. 1892.
Collection of the Charles Hosmer Morse Museum of American Art, Winter Park, FL, © The Charles Hosmer Morse Foundation, Inc.

Mitteldorfer memorial window (Mt. Sinai erupting as Moses receives the 10 commandments). Mitteldorfer-Gedenkfenster (Ausbruch des Sinai-Berges, als Moses die Zehn Gebote erhält). Vitrail commémoratif Mitteldorfer (Eruption du mont Sinaï au moment où Moïse reçoit les dix commandements).
Temple Beth Ahabah, Richmond, VA.
277.6 x 140.3 cm.
1923.
Photo: Paul Kolhoff, Richmond, VA.

Leaded glass window with flowering magnolia trees and irises. Bleiverglastes Fenster mit blühenden Magnolienbäumen und Iris. Vitrail en verre au plomb au motif d'arbustes de magnolia en fleurs et d'iris.
c. 1920.
Courtesy Marchese & Co., Santa Barbara, CA.

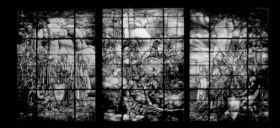

104   105

Triptych created by Tiffany for the Red Cross Headquarters at Washington, DC. Triptychon für die Zentrale des Roten Kreuzes in Washington, DC. Triptyque de Tiffany pour le siège social de la Croix Rouge à Washington, DC.
Each / Jeweils / Chacun
330 x 225 cm.
1917.

LEFT / LINKS / A GAUCHE
Saint Filomena with figures representing mercy, hope, faith and charity.
St. Filomena mit allegorischen Personifikationen für Gnade, Hoffnung, Glauben und Nächstenliebe.
Ste. Filomène et les incarnations de la grâce, de l'espoir, de la foi et de l'altruisme.

CENTER / MITTE /
AU CENTRE
Knight of the Red Cross aiding a wounded comrade.
Der Ritter des Roten Kreuzes hilft einem verwundeten Kameraden.
Le chevalier de la Croix Rouge venant en aide à un camarade blessé.

RIGHT / RECHTS /
A DROITE
Allegory of truth.
Allegorische Personifikationen der Wahrheit.
Allégorie de la vérité.

Collection of The American Red Cross, National Headquarters, Washington, DC.

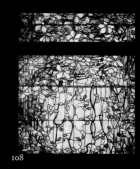

106

107

108

109

Landscape window with birch trees
and irises.
Landschaft mit Birken und Iris.
Paysage de bouleaux et d'iris.
158 x 89 cm.
c. 1917.
Christie's Images.

Lake landscape window with irises
beneath a multi-colored cloudy sky
(detail on p. 68).
Seenlandschaft mit Iris unter farbenreicher Wolkenformation
(Detail auf S. 68).
Vitrail représentant les grèves aux
iris d'un lac sous un ciel de nuages
multicolores (détail sur la p. 68).
143 x 82.5 cm.
c. 1915.
Christie's Images.

Clematis window.
Klematis-Fenster.
Vitrail au motif de clématite.
155 x 106.7 cm.
1905.
Christie's Images.

Leaded glass window with trellised
clematis vine.
Bleiverglastes Fenster mit Klema-
tisranken auf Spalier.
Vitrail en verre au plomb au motif
de clématite grimpante sur un
espalier.
287 x 151 cm.
c. 1905.
Christie's Images.

110

111

112

113

Landscape window with flowering
magnolia tree and sunset.
Landschaft mit blühendem Magno-
lienbaum vor Sonnenuntergang.
Paysage avec un arbuste de
magnolia en fleurs au coucher du
soleil.
208.2 x 110 cm.
c. 1920.
Christie's Images.

Important landscape window with
meandering stream shaded by
towering fir trees and a brilliant
sunset.
Wichtiges Landschaftsfenster mit
schattigem Bach unter hohen
Tannen vor Sonnenuntergang.
Un important vitrail d'un paysage
de ruisseau ombragé par de hauts
sapins au coucher du soleil.
87 x 66 cm.
c. 1915.
Christie's Images.

Lewis May memorial window (The
10 commandments with Mt. Zion
in the background).
Lewis-May-Gedenkfenster (Die
Zehn Gebote mit dem Berg Zion
im Hintergrund).
Vitrail en mémoire de Lewis May
(Les dix commandements avec le
temple de Salomon sur le mont
Zion en arrière-plan).
Beth-el Chapel, Temple Emanu-el,
New York.
c. 1925.
Photo: Malcolm Varon.

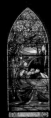

114   115   116   117

Square landscape window.
Quadratisches Landschaftsfenster.
Vitrail de paysage carré.
108.4 x 109.2 cm including frame /
mit Rahmen / avec encadrement.
Signed and dated / Signiert und
datiert / Signé et daté 1916.
Courtesy Art Focus, Zurich.

Autumn landscape window with
waterfall.
Herbstliche Landschaft mit
Wasserfall.
Paysage d'automne avec cascade.
335.3 x 259.1 cm.
Signed and dated / Signiert und
datiert / Signé et daté 1923–1924.
Collection of The Metropolitan
Museum of Art, NY; gift of Robert
W. de Forest, 1925.

Leaded glass window
(Angel of peace),
location unknown.
Bleiverglastes Fenster
(Friedensengel), un-
bekannter Ort.
Fenêtre au verre au
plomb (Ange de la
paix), localisation
inconnue.
300 x 180 cm / c. 1904.
All / alle / tous:
Courtesy Alastair
Duncan, NY.

Bradbury memorial
window (Madonna).
Bradbury-Gedenk-
fenster (Madonna).
Vitrail en mémoire de
Bradbury (Madonna).
First Congregational
Church, Augusta, ME.
c. 1880–1890.

Daniel Caldwell
Stanwood memorial
window (King David
playing the harp).
Daniel-Caldwell-Stan-
wood-Gedenkfenster
(König David beim
Harfenspiel).
Vitrail en mémoire de
Daniel Caldwell Stan-
wood (Le roi David
jouant de la harpe).
c. 1905.

118   119   120   121

Grapevine window.
Fenster mit Weinrebendekor.
Vitrail au motif de vignes
grimpantes.
248.9 x 91.4 cm.
c. 1905.
Collection of The Metropolitan
Museum of Art, NY; gift of Ruth
and Frank Stanton, 1978.

Landscape window.
Landschaftsfenster.
Vitrail de paysage.
208.5 x 74 cm.
c. 1900–1920.
Collection of The Corning Museum
of Glass, Corning, NY; gift of
Seymour Koehl and Michael
Cronin.

Leaded glass window with woman
greeting the sun.
Bleiverglastes Fenster mit einer die
Sonne begrüßenden Frau.
Fenêtre au verrre au plomb représentant une femme saluant le
soleil.
121.9 x 111.8 cm.
c. 1895.
Christie's Images.

Ornamental leaded glass window.
Ornamentales Bleiverglastes
Fenster.
Vitrail en verre au plomb d'orne-
ment.
110 x 70 cm.
c. 1900.
Courtesy Musée des Arts décora-
tifs, Paris; photo: Laurent-Sully
Jaulmes.

122

123

124

125

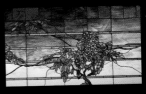

126

127

128

129

130

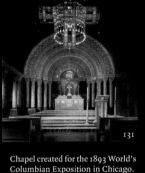

131

Winifield memorial ornamental leaded glass window, created for the Greenville Reformed Church, Jersey City, NJ.
Bleigefasstes, ornamentales Winifield-Gedenkfenster, ausgeführt für die Greenville Reformed Church, Jersey City, NJ.
Vitrail en verre au plomb d'ornement en mémoire de Winifield, créé pour la Greenville Reformed Church, Jersey City, NJ.
268 x 146 cm / c. 1890.
Christie's Images.

Fine peacock leaded glass window.
Bleiverglastes Fenster mit Pfauenmotiv.
Vitrail en verre au plomb représentant un paon.
84 x 61 cm.
c. 1910.
Christie's Images.

Arch-framed landscape window.
Rundbogenfenster mit Landschaftsmotiv.
Vitrail en plein cintre de paysage.
c. 1904.
Courtesy Alastair Duncan, NY.

Chapel created for the 1893 World's Columbian Exposition in Chicago.
Kapelle, entworfen für die World's Columbian Exposition in Chicago 1893.
Chapelle créée à l'occasion de l'Exposition Colombienne Mondiale de Chicago en 1893.
Now on view at / Heute / Aujourd'hui au: Charles Hosmer Morse Museum, Winter Park, FL.
Collection of the Charles Hosmer Morse Museum of American Art, Winter Park, FL, © The Charles Hosmer Morse Foundation, Inc.

132

133

Artisans at work in the Tiffany Studios' window workshop.
Künstler bei der Arbeit in Tiffanys Glasfensteratelier.
Artisans au travail dans l'atelier de vitraux des Tiffany Studios.
Corona, Long Island, c. 1916.
Courtesy Alastair Duncan, NY.

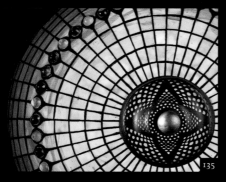

134   135   136   137

Geometric leaded and Favrile glass
and bronze table lamp (detail).
Tischlampe; bleiverglaster Lampenschirm mit geometrischem
Dekor, Bronzefuß (Detail).
Lampe de table géométrique en
verre au plomb et en bronze
(détail).
h: 71.1 cm.
Ø 55.9 cm.
c. 1910.
Christie's Images.

Table lamp with drophead blue-
eyed dragonflies (detail).
Tischlampe mit blauäugigem
Libellendekor (Detail).
Lampe de table au motif de
libellule aux yeux bleus (détail).
c. 1900.
Courtesy Macklowe Gallery, NY.

Drophead dragonfly table lamp
with an ornate bronze base.
Tischlampe mit Libellendekor und
reich verziertem Bronzefuß.
Lampe de table au motif de
libellule et au pied de bronze
ornemental.
h: 71.7 cm.
Ø 55.9 cm.
c. 1900.
Christie's Images.

138   139   140   141

Double poinsettia table lamp with
unusual root base.
Tischlampe mit Weihnachtsstern-
dekor und außergewöhnlichem
Lampenfuß in Wurzelform.
Lampe de table au motif d'une
double poinsettia avec un pied inhabituel en forme de racine.
Ø 55.9 cm.
c. 1910.
Courtesy Macklowe Gallery, NY.

Rare nasturtium table lamp with
root base.
Seltene Tischlampe in Kapuziner-
kressendekor mit Lampenfuß in
Wurzelform.
Lampe de table rare au motif de
capucine avec un pied en forme de
racine.
Ø 55.9 cm.
c. 1910.
Courtesy Macklowe Gallery, NY.

18-light lily table
lamp with bronze
lilypad base.
18-armige Tischlampe;
Schirme in Form von
Lilienblüten, Bronze-
fuß in Form von Lilien-
blättern und -stängeln.
Lampe au motif de
fleurs de lis à 18 bras
avec un pied de bronze
en forme de feuilles.
h: 52.1 cm.
c. 1900–1910.
Christie's Images.

TOP:
10-light lily lamp.
10-armige »Lilien«-
Lampe.
Lampe au motif de
fleurs de lis à 10 bras.
h: 54.9 cm.
c. 1900–1910.
Courtesy Art Focus,
Zurich.

BOTTOM:
12-light lily lamp.
12-armige »Lilien«-
Lampe.
Lampe au motif de
fleurs de lis à 12 bras.
h: 53.3 cm.
c. 1902–1910.
Courtesy Phillips
Auctioneers, NY.

142

143

144

145

Pair of 3-light lily desk lamps.
Paar dreiarmige »Lilien«-Lampen.
Deux lampes au motif de fleurs de
lis à 3 bras.
h: 32.8 cm / 21.5 cm.
c. 1905–1908.
Courtesy Phillips Auctioneers, NY.

7-light lily table lamp with bronze
lilypad base.
7-armige Tischlampe; Schirme in
Form von Lilienblüten, Bronzefuß
in Form von Lilienblättern und
-stängeln.
Lampe au motif de fleurs de lis à
7 bras avec un pied en bronze
décoré de feuilles.
h 57.1 cm.
c. 1905.
Courtesy Ophir Gallery,
Englewood, NJ.

A rare spider table lamp.
Seltene Tischlampe mit Spinnen-
netzdekor.
Lampe de table rare au motif
d'araignée.
h: 53.3 cm.
Ø 44.2 cm.
c. 1900–1910.
Christie's Images.

Pond lily table lamp with bronze
twisted vine base.
Tischlampe; Schirm mit Seerosen-
dekor, Bronzefuß in Form eines
gewundenen Weinstocks.
Lampe de table au motif de nénuphar avec un pied de vigne torsadé.
h: 68.5 cm.
Ø 52.1 cm.
c. 1900–1905.
Christie's Images.

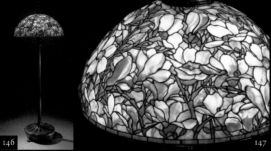

146

147

148

149

Magnolia floor lamp.
Stehlampe mit Magnoliendekor.
Lampadaire au motif de magnolia.
h: 157.5 cm.
c. 1903.
Courtesy Minna Rosenblatt
Gallery, NY.

Detail of same lamp.
Detail des Lampenschirms.
Détail du même lampadaire.

Lotus bell desk lamp.
Tischlampe; glockenförmiger
Schirm mit Lotusdekor.
Lampe de table avec un abat-jour
au motif de lotus et en forme de
cloche.
h: 53.3 cm.
c. 1905.
Courtesy Lillian Nassau
Gallery, NY.

Mandarin table lamp.
Tischlampe im Mandarin-Stil.
Lampe de table de style
« mandarin ».
h: 55.9 cm.
c. 1901.
Courtesy Macklowe Gallery, NY.

150

151

152

153

Poppy filigree floor
lamp.
Filigrane Stehlampe
mit Mohnblumen-
dekor.
Lampadaire de fili-
grane au motif de
coquelicots.
Ø 61 cm.
c. 1899–1920.
Courtesy Dennis
Marchese, CA.

Poppy table lamp on a
twisted vine base.
Tischlampe; Schirm
mit Mohnblumen-
dekor, Fuß in Form
eines gewundenen
Weinstocks.
Lampe de table au mo-
tif de coquelicots avec
un pied de vigne ondulé.
h: 50.8 cm / c. 1910.
Courtesy Dennis
Marchese, CA.

Wire mesh poppy
table lamp.
Tischlampe mit Mohn-
blumendekor in fili-
graner Bronze-
montierung.
Lampe de table au
motif de coquelicots
enlacé et en tissu
métallique.
h: 43.2 cm / c. 1900.
Courtesy Macklowe
Gallery, NY.

Spreading cherry table lamp.
Tischlampe mit Kirschblüten-
dekor.
Lampe de table au motif de cérisier
en fleurs.
h: 74.9 cm.
Ø 63.5 cm.
c. 1899–1920.
Courtesy Minna Rosenblatt
Gallery, NY.

Wisteria table lamp.
Tischlampe mit Blauregen-
(Glyzinien)-Dekor.
Lampe de table avec abat-jour au
motif de glycine.
h: 71.1 cm.
Ø 47 cm.
c. 1902.
Courtesy Art Focus, Zurich.

154

155

156

157

Elaborate grape table lamp.
Kunstvoll gearbeitete Tischlampe
mit Weintraubendekor.
Lampe de table sophistiquée au
motif de grappe de raisins.
h: 53.3 cm.
c. 1900–1905.
Courtesy Lillian Nassau
Gallery, NY.

Shade of a flowering lotus table
lamp.
Lampenschirm einer Tischleuchte
mit Lotusdekor.
Abat-jour d'une lampe de table au
motif de lotus en fleurs.
h: 47 cm.
c. 1903.
Courtesy Macklowe Gallery, NY.

Pair of desk lamps.
Paar Schreibtischlampen.
Deux lampes de bureau.
h: 41.9 cm.
c. 1910.
Courtesy Art Focus, Zurich.

Pineapple table lamp with 5 Favrile
glass shades and bronze base.
Tischlampe mit Ananasdekor und
5 Favrile-Glasschirmen, Bronzefuß.
Lampe de table en forme d'ananas
à 5 abat-jour en verre Favrile et
pied de bronze.
h: 82.5 cm.
total Ø 60 cm.
c. 1905–1910.
Courtesy Phillips Auctioneers, NY.

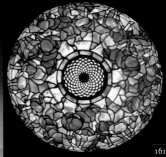

158   159   160   161

Reading lamp.
Leselampe.
Lampe d'études.
h: 61 cm.
Ø 29 cm.
c. 1900.
Courtesy Phillips Auctioneers, NY.

Double reading lamp with Moorish
shades.
Leselampe mit zwei Schirmen im
maurischen Stil.
Lampe d'études à double abat-jour
maure.
h: 57.5 cm.
c. 1898.
Courtesy Phillips Auctioneers, NY.

Tulip table lamp on bronze base
with turtleback tile inserts.
Tischlampe; Schirm mit Tulpendekor, Bronzefuß mit Schildpatteinlagen.
Lampe de table au motif de tulipe
et au pied de bronze incrusté
d'écailles.
h: 57.1 cm.
Ø 40.6 cm.
c. 1906.
Christie's Images.

View of the lamp shade from
above.
Aufsicht auf den Lampenschirms.
Vue d'en haut de l'abat-jour.

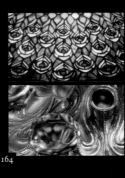

162   163   164   165

Tyler table lamp.
»Tyler«-Tischlampe.
Lampe de table
«Tyler».
h: 63.5 cm.
Ø 45.8 cm.
c. 1905–1907.
Private collection.

Right page / Rechte
Seite / Page de droite:

Bottom / Unten /
En bas
Greek key table lamp.

Tischlampe mit
Mäanderdekor.
Lampe de table en
décor méandre.
h: 45.7 cm / c. 1907.
Courtesy Macklowe
Gallery, NY.

Center / Mitte /
Au centre
Swirling leaf table
lamp.
Tischlampe mit
Blätterwirbeldekor.
Lampe de table en

style de tourbillon de
feuilles.
h: 71 cm / c. 1905.
Courtesy Phillips
Auctioneers, NY.

Top / Oben / En haut
Acorn table lamp.
Tischlampe mit
Eicheldekor.
Lampe de table au
motif de gland.
h: 58.4 cm / c. 1910
Courtesy Phillips
Auctioneers, NY.

Details of the shade (top) and the
base (bottom).
Details des Lampenschirms (oben)
und des -fußes (unten).
Détails de l'abat-jour (en haut) et
du pied (en bas).

One-of-a-kind peacock centerpiece
table lamp.
Tischlampe und Tafelaufsatz mit
Pfauenfederndekor (Unikat).
Lampe de table unique au motif de
plumes de paon.
h: 61 cm.
Ø (shade and base) 66 cm.
c. 1898.
Courtesy Phillips Auctioneers, NY.

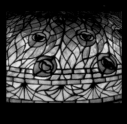

166

167

168

169

Peacock table lamp.
Tischlampe mit Pfauenfederndekor.
Lampe de table au motif de plumes
de paon.
h: 45.7 cm.
ca. 1905.
Courtesy Macklowe Gallery, NY.

A different peacock table lamp
(detail).
Detail einer anderen Tischlampe
mit Pfauenfederndekor.
Autre lampe de table au motif de
plumes de paon (détail).
h: 45.7 cm.
c. 1900.
Courtesy Macklowe Gallery, NY.

Geometric leaded glass and bronze
table lamp.
Tischlampe; bleiverglaster Lampenschirm mit geometrischem
Dekor, Bronzefuß.
Lampe de table géométrique en
verre au plomb et en bronze.
h: 85 cm.
∅ 48.2 cm.
Courtesy Phillips Auctioneers, NY.

Linen-fold desk lamp.
Schreibtischlampe mit gefälteltem
Textilschirm.
Lampe de bureau avec abat-jour
en lin.
h: 43.1 cm.
c. 1920.
Courtesy Phillips Auctioneers, NY.

170

171

172

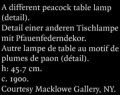

173

A collection of Tiffany Studios desk
lamps.
Verschiedene Schreibtischlampen
mit Schgirmen aus Favrile-Glas aus
den Tiffany Studios.
Collection de lampes de bureau des
Tiffany Studios; abat-jour en verre
Favrile.

Belted dogwood table lamp.
Tischlampe mit Hornstrauchdekor.
Lampe de table au motif de
cornouiller.
h: 74 cm.
∅ 51 cm.
c. 1905.
Courtesy Phillips Auctioneers, NY.

Belted dogwood table lamp.
Tischlampe mit Hornstrauchdekor.
Lampe de table au motif de
cornouiller.
h: 40.6 cm.
c. 1905.
Courtesy Macklowe Gallery, NY.

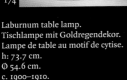

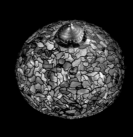

174

175

176

177

Laburnum table lamp.
Tischlampe mit Goldregendekor.
Lampe de table au motif de cytise.
h: 73.7 cm.
∅ 54.6 cm.
c. 1900–1910.
Courtesy Art Focus, Zurich.

LEFT / LINKS / A GAUCHE
Laburnum floor lamp.
Stehlampe mit Goldregendekor.
Lampadaire au motif de cytise.
∅ 55.9 cm.
c. 1903.
Courtesy Macklowe Gallery, NY.

RIGHT / RECHTS / A DROITE
Detail of the lamp shade on p. 174.
Detail des Lampenschirms auf
S. 174.
Détail de l'abat-jour à la p. 174.

Top view of the lamp shade at the
right.
Aufsicht auf den Lampenschirm
rechts.
Vue d'en haut de l'abat-jour à
droite.

RIGHT / RECHTS / A DROITE
Poppy floor lamp with gilt bronze
base; the largest shade made by
Tiffany Studios.
Stehlampe mit Mohnblumendekor
und vergoldetem Bronzefuß; der

größte jemals von den Tiffany
Studios hergestellte Lampenschirm.
Lampadaire au motif de coquelicots et au pied de bronze doré, le
plus grand abat-jour confectionné
par les Tiffany Studios.
h: 140.3 cm.
∅ 77.4 cm.
c. 1905.
Christie's Images.

178

179

180

181

TOP / OBEN / EN HAUT
Peony table lamp.
Tischlampe mit
Pfingstrosendekor.
Lampe de table au
motif de pivoine.
h: 83.8 cm.
∅ 57 cm.
c. 1905–1908.
Courtesy Art Focus,
Zurich.

BOTTOM / UNTEN /
EN BAS
Elaborate peony table
lamp.
Kunstvolle Tischlampe
mit Pfingstrosen-
dekor.
Lampe de table
sophistiqué au motif
de pivoine.
h: 55.9 cm.
c. 1901.
Courtesy Macklowe
Gallery, NY.

RIGHT / RECHTS /
A DROITE
Peony floor lamp.
Stehlampe mit
Pfingstrosendekor.
Lampadaire au motif
de pivoine.
h: 162.6 cm.
c. 1900–1910.
Courtesy Ophir Gal-
lery, Englewood, NJ.

Detail of the lamp shade at the
right.
Detail des Lampenschirms rechts.
Détail de l'abat-jour à droite.

Unusual fruit table lamp.
Außergewöhnliche Tischlampe mit
Früchtedekor.
Lampe de table insolite au motif de
fruits unique.
h: 73 cm.
∅ 61 cm.
c. 1900–1915.
Christie's Images.

182   183   184   185

Lily pad table lamp.
Tischlampe mit Seerosenblätter-
dekor.
Lampe de table au motif de feuilles
de nénuphar.
h: 61 cm.
Ø 50.8 cm.
c. 1905–1910.
Courtesy Art Focus, Zurich.

Bamboo leaded glass and bronze
table lamp.
Tischlampe mit bleiverglastem
Schirm und Bronzefuß mit Bam-
busdekor.
Lampe de table de verre au plomb
et de bronze au motif de bambou.
h: 57.1 cm.
Ø 40.8 cm.
c. 1905–1910.
Christie's Images.

Shade of a hydrangea floor lamp.
Lampenschirm einer Stehleuchte
mit Hortensiendekor.
Abat-jour d'un lampadaire au motif
d'hortensia.
Ø 66 cm.
c. 1905.
Courtesy Macklowe Gallery, NY.

186   187   188   189

Top / Oben / En haut
Pair of tulip-form
Favrile glass sconces.
Paar Wandlampen mit
Favrile-Glasschirmen
in Tulpenform.
Deux appliques de
verre Favrile en forme
de tulipes.
h: 30.5 cm.
w: 32 cm.

Bottom / Unten /
En bas
Pair of sconces.
Paar Wandlampen.
Deux appliques.
h: 45.7 cm.
c. 1910.
Courtesy Phillips
Auctioneers, NY.

Glass sconce.
Wandlampe mit Glas-
schirmen.
Applique de verre.
h: 31 cm.
c. 1910.
Courtesy Phillips
Auctioneers, NY.

Venetian table lamp with gilt
bronze base.
Venezianische Tischlampe mit
vergoldetem Bronzefuß.
Lampe de table vénitienne au pied
de bronze doré.
h: 55.9 cm.
c. 1915.
Courtesy Doyle, NY.

Zodiac table lamp with turtleback
tile inserts.
Tischlampe mit Tierkreiszeichen
und Schildpatteinlegearbeiten.
Lampe de table avec signes du
zodiaque et incrustée d'écailles.
h: 81.3 cm.
c. 1905.
Courtesy Minna Rosenblatt
Gallery, NY .

191

192

border floor lamp.
mpe; Schirm am Rand mit
rosendekor.
daire au motif de pivoine sur
ure de l'abat-jour.
cm.
1.

sy Art Focus, Zurich.

Detail of a similar peony floor
lamp.
Detail eines ähnlichen Lampen-
schirms mit Pfingstrosendekor.
Détail d'un abat-jour au motif de
pivoine similaire.
Ø 61 cm.
Courtesy Marchese & Co.,
Santa Barbara, CA.

Filigree Moorish table lamp.
Filigrane Tischlampe im
maurischen Stil.
Lampe de table en filigrane de style
maure.
h: 40.6 cm.
c. 1895.
Courtesy Marchese & Co., Santa
Barbara, CA.

Dandelion lamp on enamel ba
Tischlampe mit Löwenzahnde
emaillierter Fuß.
Lampe de table au motif de pis
lit au pied d'émail.
h: 59 cm.
Ø 22.8 cm.
c. 1900.
Courtesy Macklowe Gallery, N

195

196

s leaded glass table lamp
nze and mosaic base, one
hree known to exist.
Tischlampe; bleiverglaster
mit Lotusdekor, Bronzefuß
aikverzierung, eines von
bekannten Exemplaren.
e table très rare de verre au
motif de lotus et au pied
e et de mosaïque; il n'en
e trois exemplaires.
n / Ø 63.5 cm.
910.
ollection.

nportant pink lotus table
bron e and mo ai

Tiffany's most expensive model:
$750 when made; 1997 sold at
auction at Christie's, NY, for
$2,807,500.
Bedeutende Tischlampe mit Rosa-
Lotusdekor, Bronzefuß mit Mosaikverzierung; teuerste Tiffanylampe:
laut Katalog $750; bei Christie's,
NY, 1997 für $2 807 500 versteigert.
Lampe de table éminente au motif
de lotus rose et au pied de bronze
et de mosaïque; la lampe Tiffany la
plus onéreuse: au catalogue $750;
lors d'une vente aux enchères en 1997
chez Christie's, NY, $2 807 500.
c. 1900–1910 / Courtesy Minna

Detail of the lamp shade at the
right.
Detail des Lampenschirms rechts.
Détail de l'abat-jour à droite.

Rare red lotus table lamp with
bronze and mosaic base.
Seltene Tischlampe; Schirm mit
Roter-Lotusdekor, Bronzefuß m
Mosaikverzierung.
Lampe de table au motif de lotu
rouge rare au pied de bronze et
mosaïque.
c. 1900–1910.
h: 86.3 cm.
Ø 63.5 cm.
Christie's Images.

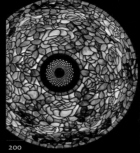

198

199

200

201

Cyclamen leaded glass and bronze table lamp.
Tischlampe; bleiverglaster Schirm mit Alpenveilchendekor, Bronzefuß.
Lampe de table au motif de cyclamen en verre au plomb et en bronze.
h: 43.2 cm.
c. 1903.
Courtesy Macklowe Gallery, NY.

TOP / OBEN / EN HAUT
Tulip table lamp with turtleback tiles.
Tischlampe mit Tulpendekor und Schildpatteinlagen.
Lampe de table au motif de tulipe et incrustée d'écailles.
h: 40.6 cm.
c. 1905.
Courtesy Ophir Gallery, Englewood, NJ.

BOTTOM / UNTEN / EN BAS
Wild rose border table lamp with ornate base.
Tischlampe; Schirmrand mit Wildrosendekor, reich verzierter Fuß.
Lampe de table au motif de rose sauvage sur la bordure de l'abatjour; pied de bronze ornemental.
h: 54.6 cm / Ø 40.6 cm.
c. 1910–1915 / Courtesy Phillips Auctioneers, NY.

View from above of the lamp at right.
Aufsicht auf die Lampe rechts.
Vue d'en haut de la lampe à droite.

Rose table lamp with turtleback tile inserts in bronze base.
Tischlampe; Schirm mit Rosendekor, Bronzefuß mit Schildpatteinlagen.
Lampe de table au motif de rose au pied de bronze incrusté d'écailles.
h: 80 cm.
Ø 62.9 cm.
c. 1915.
Christie's Images.

202

203

204

205

LEFT / LINKS / A GAUCHE
Harp-arm desk lamp.
Schreibtischlampe mit elegant geschwungener Schirmhalterung.
Lampe de bureau au manche en forme de harpe.
h: 61 cm.
Ø 25.4 cm.
c. 1904.
Courtesy Phillips Auctioneers, NY.

CENTER / MITTE / AU CENTRE
Bell table lamp.
Glockenförmige Tischlampe.
Lampe de table en forme de cloche.
h: 47 cm.
Ø 16.5 cm.
c. 1903.
Courtesy Art Focus, Zurich.

RIGHT / RECHTS / A DROITE
Desk lamp.
Schreibtischlampe.
Lampe de bureau.
h: 57.5 cm.
Ø 25.4 cm.
c. 1900.
Courtesy Phillips Auctioneers, NY.

Group of Favrile glass and bronze objects: a pair of gilt bronze and Favrile glass candlesticks (h: 33 cm); zodiac harp-arm table lamp (h: 33.6 cm); glass desklamp (h: 43.2 cm); Favrile glass and gilt bronze vase (h: 34.4 cm).
Diverse Lampen und Leuchter aus Favrile-Glas und Bronze: zwei Kerzenständer aus vergoldeter Bronze und Favrile-Glas (h: 33 cm); Tischlampe mit geschwungener Halterung und Tierkreiszeichen (h: 33,6 cm); Schreibtischlampe mit Glas-

schirm (h: 43,2 cm); Vase aus Favrile-Glas und vergoldeter Bronze (h: 34,4 cm).
Ensemble de lampes en verre Favrile et de bronze: deux chandeliers en bronze doré et en verre Favrile (h: 33 cm); lampe de table au manche en forme de harpe avec signes du zodiaque (h: 33,6 cm); lampe de bureau en verre (h: 43,2 cm); vase de verre Favrile et de bronze doré (h: 34,4 cm).
Courtesy Phillips Auctioneers, NY.

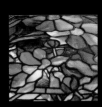

206

207

208

209

Detail of the lamp shade at the right.
Detail des Lampenschirms rechts.
Détail de l'abat-jour à droite.

Peony table lamp with mosaic base.
Tischlampe mit Pfingstrosendekor auf Mosaikfuß.
Lampe de table au motif de pivoine au pied de mosaïque.
h: 55.9 cm.
c. 1902.
Courtesy Macklowe Gallery, NY.

Leaded glass and gilt bronze tulip table lamp.
Bleiverglaste Tischlampe mit Tulpendekor auf vergoldetem Bronzefuß.
Lampe de table au motif de tulipe en verre au plomb et en bronze doré.
h: 58.4 cm.
c. 1905–1908.
Courtesy Doyle, NY.

Daffodil with dogwood border table lamp with gilt bronze base.
Tischlampe mit vergoldetem Bronzefuß; Lampenschirm mit Osterglockendekor und Hornstrauch-Bordüre.
Lampe de table au motif de jonquille et de cornouiller en bordure; pied de bronze doré.
h: 68.6 cm.
c. 1905–1908.
Courtesy Doyle, NY.

210

211

212

213

Daffodil table lamp with stylized bronze base.
Tischlampe mit Osterglockendekor und stilisiertem Bronzefuß.
Lampe de table au motif de jonquille et au pied de bronze stylisé.
h: 53.3 cm.
c. 1910–1915.
Courtesy Phillips Auctioneers, NY.

Detail of the lamp shade.
Detail des Lampenschirms.
Détail de l'abat-jour.

Daffodil table lamp on footed bronze base.
Tischlampe mit Osterglockendekor und gefußtem Bronzesockel.
Lampe de table au motif de jonquille au socle de bronze à pieds.
h: 40.6 cm.
c. 1901.
Courtesy Macklowe Gallery, NY.

Daffodil and narcissus table lamp.
Tischlampe mit Osterglocken- und Narzissendekor.
Lampe de table au motif de jonquille et de narcisse.
h: 73.7 cm.
Ø 50.8 cm.
c. 1905.
Courtesy Art Focus, Zurich.

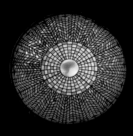

214

215

216

217

Aztec geometric lampshade.
Lampenschirm in geometrischem Aztekendekor.
Abat-jour géométrique de style aztèque.
Ø 63.5 cm.
c. 1910.
Courtesy Ophir Gallery, Englewood, NJ.

TOP LEFT / OBEN LINKS / EN HAUT A GAUCHE
Geometric table lamp with balls.
Geometrische Tischlampe mit Kugeln.
Lampe de table géométrique avec des boules.
h: 55.9 cm.
c. 1910.
Courtesy Dennis Marches, CA.

TOP RIGHT / OBEN RECHTS / EN HAUT A DROITE
Geometric table lamp.
Geometrische Tischlampe.
Lampe de table géométrique.
h: 78.6 cm.
Ø 62 cm.
c. 1900–1908.
Courtesy Phillips Auctioneers, NY.

BOTTOM LEFT / UNTEN LINKS / EN BAS A GAUCHE
Greek key table lamp.
Tischlampe mit Mäandermuster.
Lampe de table avec motif de méandre.
h: 64.8 cm.
Ø 50.8 cm.
c. 1902.
Courtesy Phillips Auctioneers, NY.

BOTTOM RIGHT / UNTEN RECHTS / EN BAS A DROITE
Unusual herringbone table lamp.
Außergewöhnliche Tischlampe mit Fischgrätenmuster.
Lampe de table inhabituel au motif de chevrons.
h: 30.5 cm.
c. 1910.
Courtesy Ophir Gallery, Englewood, NJ.

LEFT / LINKS / A GAUCHE
Pomegranate table lamp.
Tischlampe mit Granatapfeldekor.
Lampe de table au motif de grenade.
h: 40.6 cm.
c. 1910.
Courtesy Ophir Gallery, Englewood, NJ.

RIGHT / RECHTS / A DROITE
Mushroom table lamp.
Tischlampe mit Pilzdekor.
Lampe de table au motif de champignon.
h: 56 cm.
Ø 40.5 cm.
c. 1898.
Courtesy Phillips Auctioneers, NY.

Acorn table lamp with glass inserts in base.
Tischlampe mit Eicheldekor.
Lampe de table au motif de gland.
h: 59 cm.
Ø 45.7 cm.
c. 1910.
Courtesy Phillips Auctioneers, NY.

218

219

Group of Favrile glass and bronze lamps and candlesticks.
Gruppe von Tischlampen und Kerzenleuchtern aus Favrile-Glas und Bronze.
Ensemble de lampes de verre Favrile et de bronze ainsi que deux chandeliers.
Courtesy Phillips Auctioneers, NY.

221

222

223

Favrile glass table lamp.
n-Tischlampe aus Favrile-

e table à pétrole.
m.

Phillips Auctioneers, NY.

Rare pebble table lamp combining leaded glass, stone, bronze and blown glass.
Seltene Tischlampe; bleiverglaster Schirm mit Kieseldekor, Fuß aus Stein, Bronze und freigeblasenem Glas.
Lampe de table rare au décor de cailloux, en verre au plomb, en pierre, en bronze et en verre marron.
h: 41.9 cm / Ø 36.8 cm.
c. 1904–1910.
Christie's Images.

Rare dragonfly table lamp combining leaded glass, stone, bronze and blown glass.
Seltene Tischlampe; bleiverglaster Schirm mit Libellendekor, Fuß aus Stein, Bronze und freigeblasenem Glas.
Lampe de table au motif de libellule en verre au plomb, en pierre, en bronze et en verre marron.
h: 47 cm / Ø 36.8 cm / c. 1900.
Christie's Images.

View of the same lamp from above.
Aufsicht auf die gleiche Lampe.
Vue d'en haut de la même lampe.

225

226

227

er table lamp.
pe mit Glockenblumen-

e table au motif de
le.

Phillips Auctioneers, NY.

Woodbine foliage table lamp.
Tischlampe mit Jungfernreben-dekor.
Lampe de table au motif de feuilles de vigne sauvage.
h: 66 cm.
Ø 51.4 cm.
c. 1915.
Courtesy Art Focus, Zurich.

Three Favrile glass and bronze candlestick lamps.
Drei Kerzenleuchter aus Favrile-Glas mit Bronzefüßen.
Trois lampes en forme de chandelier en verre Favrile et en

CENTER / MITTEL /
AU CENTRE
Glass and ceramic table lamp.
Tischlampe aus Glas und Keramik.
Lampe de table en verre et en céramique.
h: 52.4 cm.

RIGHT / RECHTS /
A DROITE
Damascene table lamp.
Tischlampe in damaszenischem Stil.
Lampe de table damassée.
h: 35.6 cm.

229 230 231

…vrile glass and bronze
…mps.
…hreibtischlampen aus
…Glas und Bronze.
…mpes de bureau en verre
…et en bronze.
… cm / 57.5 cm.

…y Phillips Auctioneers, NY.

Favrile glass and bronze candlestick lamp.
Kerzenleuchter aus Favrile-Glas
und Bronze.
Chandelier en verre Favrile et en
bronze.
h: 44.3 cm.
c. 1902.
Courtesy Art Focus, Zurich.

"October light" hanging lamp
(detail).
»Oktoberlicht«-Hängelampe
(Detail).
Lustre « lumière d'octobre »
(détail).
∅ 63.5 cm.
c. 1910–1915.
Courtesy Ophir Gallery,
Englewood, NJ.

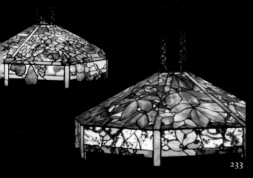

233 234 23…

…ium on trellis hanging

…ampe mit rankendem
…nerkressedekor.
…u motif de capucines
…ntes.
… cm.

Autumn leaves hanging lamp.
Hängelampe mit Herbstblattdekor.
Lustre au motif de feuilles
d'automne.
∅ 63.5 cm.
c. 1903.
Courtesy Macklowe Gallery, NY.

Rare trumpet creeper hanging
lamp.
Seltene Hängelampe mit Trompe-
tenblumendekor.
Lustre rare au motif de trompette
de Jérico.
∅ 71.1 cm.
c. 1903.

Trumpet creeper leaded glass and
bronze table lamp with fractured
glass ground.
Bleiverglaste Tischlampe auf Bron
zefuß mit Trompetenblumendeko
auf Craquelé-Glasgrund.
Lampe de table au motif de
trompette de Jérico en verre au

6

238

237

23

...ly hanging lamp.
...he Deckenlampe.
...tre des débuts de Tiffany.
...60 cm.
....3.5 cm.
...889–1910.
...urtesy Phillips Auctioneers, NY.

Hanging Favrile glass tile lanterns
with turtleback inserts.
Deckenlaternen aus Favrile-Glas
mit Schildpatteinlagen.
Lanternes en verre incrustées
d'écailles.
l: 34.3 cm.
Chains / Ketten / chaînes: 127 cm.
c. 1898–1920.
Courtesy Macklowe Gallery, NY.

Moorish-style chandelier with
turtleback tiles.
Hängelampe mit Schildpatteinlagen im maurischen Stil.
Lustre de style maure incrusté
d'écailles.
h: 96.5 cm.
Ø 54.5 cm.
c. 1899–1920.
Courtesy Phillips Auctioneers, NY.

Hanging lantern with turtleback
insets.
Deckenlaterne mit Schildpatteinlagen.
Lanterne incrustée d'écailles.
h: 81.3 cm.
c. 1901.
Courtesy Macklowe Gallery, NY.

...0

241

242

...2.

...agonfly table lamp with mosaic
...se.
...chlampe mit Libellendekor und
...saikfuß.
...npe de table au motif de
...llule et au pied de mosaïque.
...3.2 cm.
...900.
...rtesy Macklowe Gallery, NY.

Dragonfly hanging lamp.
Hängelampe mit Libellendekor.
Lustre au motif de libellule.
Ø 72.4 cm.
1899–1920.
Courtesy Macklowe Gallery, NY.

Dogwood cone-shaped hanging
lamp.
Kegelförmige Hängeleuchte mit
Hornstrauchdekor.
Plafonnier conique au motif de
cornouiller.
Ø 71.1 cm.
c. 1904.
Courtesy Macklowe Gallery, NY.

Dogwood hanging lamp.
Hängelampe mit Hornstrauchdekor.
Lustre au motif de cornouiller.
Ø 72.4 cm.
c. 1903.
Courtesy Macklowe Gallery, NY.

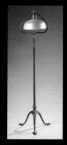

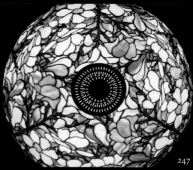

244

245

248

249

LEFT / LINKS / A GAUCHE
Harp-arm tripod floor lamp.
Dreifüßige Stehlampe mit
geschwungener Halterung.
Lampadaire à trois pieds au
manche en forme de harpe.
h: 140 cm.
Ø 25.5 cm.
c. 1910–1915.
Courtesy Phillips Auctioneers, NY.

RIGHT / RECHTS / A DROITE
Linen-fold floor lamp.
Stehlampe mit gefälteltem
Textilschirm.
Lampadaire avec un abat-jour
en lin.
h: 151 cm.
Ø 24 cm.
c. 1915–1920.
Courtesy Phillips Auctioneers, NY.

LEFT / LINKS / A GAUCHE
Harp-arm floor lamp.
Stehlampe mit geschwungener
Halterung.
Lampadaire au manche en forme
de harpe.
h: 139.8 cm.
Ø 26 cm.
c. 1910–1915.
Courtesy Phillips Auctioneers, NY.

RIGHT / RECHTS / A DROITE
Harp-arm damascene floor lamp.
Stehlampe mit geschwungener
Halterung im damaszenischen Stil.
Lampadaire damassé au manche
en forme de harpe.
h: 140 cm.
c. 1910–1915.
Courtesy Phillips Auctioneers, NY.

Blue magnolia floor lamp.
Blaue-Magnolien-Stehlampe.
Lampadaire au motif de magnolia
bleu.
h: 195.6 cm.
Ø 71.1 cm.
c. 1905.
Christie's Images.

View of the same lamp from above.
Aufsicht auf die gleiche Lampe.
Vue d'en haut de la même lampe.

Six-light Favrile glass and bronze
candelabra.
Sechsarmiger Kandelaber aus
Favrile-Glas und Bronze.
Candélabre à six bras en verre
Favrile et en bronze.
h: 39.4 cm.
l: 55.9 cm.
c. 1910.
Courtesy Art Focus, Zurich.

250

251

252

253

Detail of the lamp shade at the
right.
Detail des Lampenschirms rechts.
Détail de l'abat-jour à droite.

Yellow lotus leaded glass and
bronze chandelier.
Bleiverglaste Hängelampe mit
Gelber-Lotus-Dekor in Bronze-
montierung.
Lustre au motif de lotus jaune en
verre au plomb et en bronze.
Ø 74.9 cm.
Undated.
Christie's Images.

Shade of a leaded glass and filigree
red poppy floor lamp.
Bleiverglaster Lampenschirm einer
Stehlampe; Mohnblumendekor mit
Filigranarbeit.
Abat-jour d'un lampadaire au motif
en filigrane de coquelicots.
Ø 61 cm.
c. 1899–1920.
Courtesy Dennis Marchese, CA.

254 255   256   257

From: Six Favrile glass vases, those
on the extreme left and right with
applied glass trailings (detail of
p. 292/293).
Sechs Vasen aus Favrile-Glas, die
beiden äußeren mit applizierten
Glasauflagen (Detail von S. 292/
293).
Ensemble de six vases Tiffany, dont
le vase de gauche et de droite avec
des boursouflures appliquées
(détail de la p. 292/293).
c. 1898–1908.
Courtesy Macklowe Gallery, NY.

Favrile glass silver-mounted vase.
Vase aus Favrile-Glas in Silberfassung.
Vase de verre Favrile avec sertissure
d'argent.
h: 26.7 cm.
c. 1900.
Courtesy Phillips Auctioneers, NY.

Favrile glass vase in sterling silver
mount; probably the first vase
Tiffany made .
Vase aus Favrile-Glas in Silberfassung. Es handelt sich vermutlich
um die erste Glasvase von Tiffany.
Vase de verre Favrile avec sertissure
d'argent. Il est probablement le
premier vase fabriqué par Tiffany.
1893.
Courtesy Macklowe Gallery, NY.

258 259   260   261

Favrile glass vase with silver mount
and inlay.
Vase aus Favrile-Glas mit geschnittenem Marqueteriedekor in
Silberfassung.
Vase de verre au décor de marque-
terie avec sertissure d'argent.
c. 1896.
Courtesy Phillips Auctioneers, NY.

Three Favrile glass vases: peacock
eye (left), flower form (center), and
hearts and vine (right).
Drei Vasen aus Favrile-Glas: mit
Pfauenaugendekor (links), in
Blütenform (Mitte) und mit Blatt-
und Rankendekor (rechts).
Trois vases en verre Favrile : au
motif d'ocelles (à gauche), en
forme de fleur (au centre), au motif
de cœurs et de sarments (à droite).
c. 1900–1905.
Courtesy Macklowe Gallery, NY.

Flower-form Favrile glass vase.
Vase aus Favrile-Glas in Blüten-
form.
Vase de verre Favrile en forme de
fleur.
h: 40.6 cm.
c. 1905.
Courtesy Macklowe Gallery, NY.

262

263

264

265

266

267

268

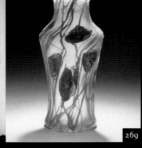

269

270

271

Watercolor sketches from a scrap book of Tiffany.
Aquarellierte Skizzen aus einem Notizbuch Tiffanys.
Ebauches à l'aquarelle dans un carnet de Tiffany.
c. 1925 / Christie's Images.

Cameo-carved paperweight vase with leaf and vine motif. The decor of the vase is caught between the interior and exterior surfaces of the glass, creating a luminescent effect.

Vase aus »Paperweight«-Favrile-Glas mit geschnittenem Blatt- und Rankendekor. Die Dekorationen sind direkt in die Glasschichten eingelegt, was den leuchtenden Effekt erzielt.
Vase de verre Favrile « paper-weight » au motif de feuillage et de sarments avec des camées sculptées. Les motifs de décoration furent incrustés dans le verre et donnent ainsi un effet luisant.
c. 1902.
Courtesy Macklowe Gallery, NY.

Three vases and a bowl, all of Favrile glass.
Drei Vasen und eine Schale aus Favrile-Glas.
Trois vases et un bol de verre Favrile.
c. 1900–1905.
Courtesy Lillian Nassau Gallery, NY.

LEFT / LINKS / A GAUCHE
Persian peacock-eye rosewater sprinkler.
Rosensprenggefäß aus Favrile-Glas mit Pfauenaugendekor.
Arroseur d'eau de rose persan au motif d'ocelles.
h: 35.6 cm / c. 1905.
Courtesy Macklowe Gallery, NY.

RIGHT / RECHTS / A DROITE
Favrile glass peacock vase.
Vase aus Favrile-Glas mit Pfauenaugendekor.
Vase de verre Favrile au motif d'ocelles.
h: 53.3 cm / 1905.
Courtesy Macklowe Gallery, NY.

272

273

274   275

TOP / OBEN / EN HAUT
Paperweight vase with gold inserts.
Vase aus »Paper-weight«-Favrile-Glas mit Goldeinlage.
Vase de verre Favrile « paperweight » avec incrustations d'or.
h: 45.7 cm / c. 1903.
Courtesy Macklowe Gallery, NY.

BOTTOM / UNTEN / EN BAS
Leaf-and-vine vase.
Vase aus Favrile-Glas mit Blatt- und Rankendekor.
Vase au motif de feuilles et sarments.
h: 30.5 cm.
c. 1905.
Courtesy Macklowe Gallery, NY.

Three flower-form Favrile glass vases.
Drei Vasen aus Fravri-le-Glas in Blüten-form.
Trois vases en forme de fleur.
h: 43.2 cm (left), 33 cm (center), 48.3 cm (right).
c. 1896–1900.
Courtesy Ophir Gal-

Production of a Favrile glass vase at the Tiffany Studios.
Herstellung einer Favrile-Glasvase in den Tiffany Studios.
Production d'un vase de verre Favrile aux Tiffany Studios.
Period photograph.
Christie's Images.

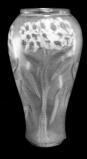

276

278

277

279

Paperweight vase Millefiori.
Vase aus »Paperweight«-Favrile-Glas mit Millefiori-Dekor.
Vase Millefiori de verre Favrile « paperweight ».
h: 38.1 cm.
1910.
Courtesy Macklowe Gallery, NY.

Exceptional Cypriot glass vase with a silver wave pattern and eight windows that reveal the

rainbow iridescent "confetti" glass interior.
Außergewöhnliche Vase aus »Cypriot«-Favrile-Glas mit silberfarbenem Wellendekor und acht »Fenstern«, die den irisierenden »Confetti«-Unterfang freilegen.
Vase de verre « Cypriot » extraordinaire avec des ondes en argent. À travers les huit vitraux apparaissent de l'intérieur les couleurs irisées de l'arc-en-ciel.
1903.
Courtesy Macklowe Gallery, NY.

Three Favrile glass vases: with applied iridescent gold glass shoulder (left); Cypriot with mottled brown texture (center); iridescent blue swirls on emerald green (right).
Drei Vasen aus Favrile-Glas: mit irisierendem Goldglas-Überfang (links), mit braunem Fleckendekor »Cypriot«-Favrile-Glas (Mitte) und mit irisierendem blauen Banddekor auf smaragdgrünem Überfang (rechts).
Trois vases de verre Favrile : à gauche avec une application en verre doré irisé, au centre vase de verre Favrile « Cypriot » avec une texture d'un brun moucheté, à droite un vase au décor de ruban bleu irisé sur une application verte émeraude.
h: 14 cm / 19.1 cm / 23.75 cm.
c. 1905–1908.
Courtesy Phillips Auctioneers, NY.

Cypriot vase with moss-green texture and irridescent gold swirls.
Vase aus »Cypriot«-Favrile-Glas mit moosgrünem Flecken- und irisierendem goldfarbenen Banddekor.
Vase de verre Favrile « Cypriot » vert mousse et aux dorures ondulées.
h: 26 cm.
c. 1910.
Courtesy Phillips Auctioneers, NY.

280

281

Gold Favrile glass Jack-in-the-pulpit vase.
»Jack-in-the-Pulpit«-Vase aus goldfarbenem Favrile-Glas.
Vase de verre Favrile en forme de « Jack-in-the-pulpit ».
h: 34.3 cm / c. 1900.
Courtesy Spencer Gallery, Palm Beach, FL.

Blue Favrile glass Jack-in-the-pulpit vase.
»Jack-in-the-Pulpit«-Vase aus blauem Favrile-Glas.
Vase de verre Favrile bleu en forme de « Jack-in-the-pulpit ».
h: 34.3 cm / c. 1900.
Courtesy Macklowe Gallery, NY.

Gold Favrile glass Jack-in-the-pulpit vase.
»Jack-in-the-Pulpit«-Vase aus goldfarbenem Favrile-Glas.
Vase de verre Favrile doré en forme de Jack-in-the-pulpit.
h: 53.3 cm.
c. 1900.
Courtesy Lillian Nassau Gallery, NY.

282   283   284   285

Three Favrile glass vases: gold
jack-in-the-pulpit vase (left), small
round vase (center), and peacock
eye cypriot vase (right).
Drei Vasen aus Favrile-Glas: gold-
farbene »Jack-in-the-Pulpit«-Vase
(links), kleine Kugelvase (Mitte)
und Vase aus »Cypriote«-Favrile-
Glas mit Pfauenaugendekor.
Trois vases de verre Favrile : vase
doré en forme de « Jack-in-the-
pulpit » (à gauche), petit vase rond
(au centre) ; vase de verre Favrile
« Cypriot » à ocelles (à droite).

h: 50,8 cm / 8,9 cm / 38,1 cm.
c. 1903–1905.
Courtesy Macklowe Gallery, NY.

Favrile glass vase with bronze foot.
Vase aus Favrile-Glas mit Bronzefuß.
Vase de verre Favrile au pied de
bronze.
h: 16.5 cm.
c. 1900.
Courtesy Macklowe Gallery, NY.

Favrile glass vases: flower-form (l),
paperweight with leaf and vines (2nd
fr l), green iridescent swirls (2nd
fr r), and with leaf-and-vine decor.
Vasen aus Favrile-Glas: in Blüten-
form (l), in »Paperweight«-Favrile-
Glas mit Blatt und Rankendekor
(M l), mit irisierendem Banddekor
(M r) und mit Blatt- und Rankendekor.
Vases de verre Favrile: en forme de
fleurs (à g.); en verre Favrile « paperweight » avec un décor de feuilles et
de sarments (centre à gauche); avec

un décor de ruban irisé (centre à
droite) et de feuilles et sarments.
c. 1898–1905.
Courtesy Macklowe Gallery, NY.

Rare midnight blue Favrile glass
vase with bands of iridescent green.
Seltene Vase aus mitternachts-
blauem Favrile-Glas mit grün
irisierendem Banddekor.
Vase rare bleu de nuit de verre Favrile
au décor de ruban vertement irisé.
h: 26.7 cm / c. 1898.
Courtesy Macklowe Gallery, NY.

286   287   288   289

LEFT / LINKS / A GAUCHE
Flowered paperweight
Favrile glass vase.
Vase aus »Paper-
weight«-Favrile-Glas
mit Blütendekor.
Vase de verre Favrile
« paperweight » au
motif de fleurs.
h: 22.9 cm.
c. 1904.
Courtesy Ophir Gal-
lery, Englewood, NJ.

RIGHT / RECHTS /
A DROITE
Favrile glass lava vase.
Vase aus »Lava«-
Favrile-Glas.
Vase de verre Favrile
« pierre de lave ».
c. 1907.
Courtesy Ophir Gal-
lery, Englewood, NJ.

Cameo Favrile glass
vase.
Vase aus geschnitte-
nem Favrile-Glas, so-
genanntes »Cameo«-
Glas.
Vase de verre Favrile
coupé, dit verre de
camée.
h: 20.3 cm.
c. 1905.
Courtesy Ophir Gal-
lery, Englewood, NJ.

LEFT / LINKS / A GAUCHE
Onion-form Favrile
glass vase.
Vase aus Favrile-Glas
in Zwiebelform.
Vase de verre Favrile
en forme d'oignon.
h: 33 cm.
c. 1906.
Courtesy Macklowe
Gallery, NY.

RIGHT / RECHTS /
A DROITE
Paperweight Favrile
glass vase with leaves.
Vase aus »Paper-
weight«-Favrile-Glas
mit Blattdekor.
Vase de verre Favrile
« paperweight » au
motif de feuilles.
c. 1906.
Both / Beide / Les deux
Courtesy Ophir Gal-
lery, Englewood, NJ.

Paperweight Favrile
glass vase with moss-
green and burgundy
swirls.
Vase aus »Paper-
weight«-Favrile-Glas
mit moosgrünem und
burgunderfarbenem
Banddekor.
Vase de verre Favrile
« paperweight » au
décor de ruban vert
mousse et bordeaux.
c. 1904.

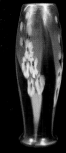

290   291   292   293

Watercolor sketches from a scrap book of Tiffany.
Aquarellierte Skizzen aus einem Notizbuch Tiffanys.
Ebauches à l'aquarelle dans un carnet de Tiffany.
1925.
Christie's Images.

Paperweight Favrile glass vase with flowers.
Vase aus »Paperweight«-Favrile-Glas mit Blütendekor.
Vase de verre Favrile « paperweight » au motif de fleurs.
h: 27.9 cm.
c. 1905.
Courtesy Macklowe Gallery, NY.

Six Favrile glass vases, those on the extreme left and right with applied glass trailings (detail on p. 254/255).
Sechs Vasen aus Favrile-Glas, die beiden äußeren mit applizierten Glasauflagen (Detail auf S. 254/255).
Ensemble de six vases Tiffany, dont le vase de gauche et de droite avec des boursouflures appliquées (détail à la p. 254/255).
c. 1898–1908.
Courtesy Macklowe Gallery, NY.

294   295   296   297

Blue Favrile glass onion-form vase.
Vase aus blauem Favrile-Glas in Zwiebelform.
Vase de verre Favrile bleu en forme d'oignon.
c. 1904.
Courtesy Spencer Gallery, Palm Beach, FL.

Aquamarine Favrile glass vase.
Vase aus »Aquamarine«-Favrile-Glas.
Vase de verre Favrile « aigue-marine ».
c. 1910.
Courtesy Lillian Nassau Gallery, NY.

Paperweight Favrile glass vase with anemones.
Vase aus »Paperweight«-Favrile-Glas mit Anemonendekor.
Vase de verre Favrile « paperweight » au motif d'anémone.
h: 26.7 cm.
c. 1905.
Courtesy Ophir Gallery, Englewood, NJ.

Pair of Favrile glass intaglia leaf-and-vine vases.
Paar Vasen aus Favrile-Glas mit Blatt- und geschnittenem Rankendekor.
Deux vases de verre Favrile au motif coupé de feuilles et sarments.
h: 27.9 cm.
c. 1905.
Courtesy Macklowe Gallery, NY.

299

300

ee decorated Favrile glass
els.
Gefäße aus Favrile-Glas.
s récipients en verre Favrile.
00–1910.
tesy Phillips Auctioneers, NY

Three Favrile glass vases.
Drei Vasen aus Favrile-Glas.
Trois vases de verre Favrile.
h: 53.3 cm / 32.5 cm / 17.8 cm.
c. 1900–1910.
Courtesy Phillips Auctioneers, NY.

Pages in a photograph album of
Louis Comfort Tiffany depicting
objects from c. 1895 to c. 1912;
with handwritten notes.
Seiten aus einem Fotoalbum von
Louis Comfort Tiffany mit Bildern
von Objekten aus der Zeit von ca.
1895–ca. 1912; mit handschrift-
lichen Notizen.

Des pages d'un album de photographies de Louis Comfort Tiffan
montrant des objets d'environ 1
jusqu'à environ 1912; avec des
notes de sa main propre.
Private collection.

303

304

Favrile glass lava vases.
Vasen aus »Lava«-Favrile-

vases de verre Favrile en
re de lave ».
9 cm / 15.2 cm.
0.

Favrile glass vase with leaf motif.
Vase aus Favrile-Glas mit Blattdekor.
Vase de verre Favrile au motif de
feuilles.
h: 59.7 cm.
c. 1905.

Pair of ceramic covered vessels
(h: 24.2 cm), a ceramic vase in urn
form with 3 handles (h: 23 cm), and
five ceramic lamp bases (h: 9 cm).
Paar Deckelvasen (h: 24.2 cm), eine
dreihenkelige Vase (h: 23 cm) und
fünf Lampenfüße (h: 9 cm) aus

Deux vases à couvercle en céramique (h: 24.2 cm), un vase en
céramique en forme d'urne à troi
anses (h: 23 cm) et cinq pieds de
lampes en céramique (h: 9 cm).
c. 1905.
Courtesy Phillips Auctioneers, NY

Born in New York City on February 18, to Charles Lewis Tiffany, founder of Tiffany & Co.	1848	Am 18. Februar als Sohn von Charles Lewis Tiffany, dem Gründer von Tiffany & Co., in New York City geboren.	1848	Né à New York, le 18 février; fils de Charles Lewis Tiffany, fondateur de la Tiffany & Co.
Studies at the National Academy of Design, New York.	1866	Studiert an der National Academy of Design, New York.	1866	Il étudie à la National Academy of Design, à New York.
Informally studies painting with noted artist George Inness; exhibits paintings at the National Academy of Design, New York.	1867	Erste zwanglose Beschäftigung mit der Malerei bei George Inness; Beteiligung an einer Ausstellung in der National Academy of Design, New York.	1867	Etudie la peinture en amateur chez l'artiste réputé George Inness ; il expose des tableaux à la National Academy of Design, à New York.
While in Europe, studies painting with French academic artist Léon-Charles-Adrien Bailly.	1868– 1869	Setzt in Europa Studium der Malerei beim französischen Académie-Künstler Léon-Charles-Adrien Bailly fort.	1868– 1869	Lors de son séjour en Europe, il étudie la peinture avec l'artiste académique français Léon-Charles-Adrien Bailly.
Elected to membership in the Century Club, New York; meets painter Samuel Colman; visits Cairo, Egypt.	1870	Zum Mitglied des Century Club, New York, gewählt; lernt den Maler Samuel Colman kennen; besucht Kairo, Ägypten.	1870	Elu membre du Century Club, à New York ; il rencontre le peintre Samuel Colman ; il visite Le Caire, en Egypte.
Elected as an associate member of the National Academy of Design, New York.	1871	Zum außerordentlichen Mitglied der National Academy of Design in New York gewählt.	1871	Elu membre associé de la National Academy of Design, à New York.
Marries Mary Woodbridge Goddard on May 15.	1872	Am 15. Mai Heirat mit Mary Woodbridge Goddard.	1872	Le 15 mai, il épouse Mary Woodbridge Goddard.
Earliest experiments in glassmaking at New York's commercial glass houses. First daughter, Mary, is born on April 3rd.	1873	Führt in den New Yorker Glashütten erste Experimente mit Glas durch; am 3. April Geburt der ersten Tochter, Mary.	1873	Premières expérimentations avec la fabrication du verre aux verreries à New York; naissance de sa première fille, Mary, le 3 avril.
First son is born on December 9, but dies three weeks later.	1874	Geburt des ersten Sohns am 9. Dezember; er stirbt drei Wochen später.	1874	Le 9 décembre, naissance de son premier fils, qui décédera trois semaines plus tard.
Exhibits paintings at the Philadelphia Centennial Exposition, the National	1876	Stellt auf der Weltausstellung in Philadelphia, in der National Academy of Design	1876	Il expose à la Philadelphia Centennial Exposition, à la National Academy of

1878	Exhibits paintings at the Exposition Universelle in Paris; completes first window commission for St. Marks' Episcopal Church, Islip, New York; is elected treasurer of the Society of American Artists; son Charles Lewis Tiffany II is born on January 7.
1879	Establishes L. C. Tiffany & Associated Artists, an interior decorating business, with Candace Wheeler, Lockwood de Forest and Samuel Colman; is commissioned to decorate George Kemp's Fifth Avenue residence in New York City as well as the dining room of William H. de Forest; daughter Hilda is born on August 24.
1880	Elected to full membership in the National Academy of Design, New York; decorates library and Veteran's Room of New York's Seventh Regiment Armory, the entrance hall and stairway of the Union League Club, and the drop curtain for the Madison Square Theatre; experiments in mosaics and wallpaper design.
1881	Registers patent for opalescent glass.
1882	Executes commissions for the William S. Kimball residence, Rochester, New York; the Mark Twain residence, Hartford, Connecticut; the Cornelius Vanderbilt II mansion in New York City; the Ogden Goelet residence, Hartford, Connecticut;

1878	Beteiligt sich mit Gemälden an der Weltausstellung in Paris; für die St. Mark's Episcopal Church in Islip auf Long Island führt er seinen ersten Kirchenfensterauftrag aus; wird zum Schatzmeister der Society of American Artists gewählt; am 7. Januar Geburt seines Sohns Charles Lewis II.
1879	Gründet das Innenausstattungsunternehmen L. C. Tiffany & Associated Artists mit Candace Wheeler, Lockwood de Forest und Samuel Colman; wird mit der Innenausstattung der Villa von George Kemp in der Fifth Avenue und des Esszimmers in William H. de Forests New Yorker Wohnung beauftragt; am 24. August Geburt der zweiten Tochter, Hilda.
1880	Vollmitglied der National Academy of Design, New York; gestaltet die Bibliothek und den Veteranensaal, das Foyer und das Treppenhaus des Union League Club sowie den Bühnenvorhang für das Madison Square Theatre, alle in New York; erste Mosaik-Experimente und Tapetenentwürfe.
1881	Meldet ein Patent für Opaleszentglas an.
1882	Wird mit zahlreichen Innenausstattungen beauftragt: für die Residenzen von William S. Kimball in Rochester, New York; von Mark Twain in Hartford, Connecticut; von Cornelius Vanderbilt II. in New York; von Ogden Goelet in New York; für das Esszimmer von

1878	Il présente des tableaux à l'Exposition Universelle de Paris ; il exécute sa première commande de vitrail pour l'église épiscopale Saint Mark, à Islip, New York ; il est élu trésorier de la Society of American Artists ; le 7 janvier, naissance de son fils, Charles Lewis Tiffany II.
1879	Il fonde la L. C. Tiffany & Associated Artists, entreprise de décoration intérieure, avec Candace Wheeler, Lockwood de Forest et Samuel Colman ; reçoit une commande de décoration pour la résidence de George Kemp, sur la 5e Avenue, à New York, et pour la salle à manger de William H. de Forest ; le 24 août, naissance de sa fille Hilda.
1880	Elu membre plénier de la National Academy of Design, New York ; il décore la bibliothèque et la Veteran's Room du 7e Regiment Armory, à New York, le vestibule et l'escalier de l'Union League Club, et le rideau de scène du Madison Square Theatre ; essais de mosaïques et de motifs de papiers peints.
1881	Il fait enregistrer un brevet de verre opalin.
1882	Il exécute des commandes pour la résidence de William S. Kimball, à Rochester, New York ; pour la résidence de Mark Twain, à Hartford, Connecticut ; pour l'hôtel particulier de Cornelius Vanderbilt II à New York ; pour la résidence de Ogden Goelet, à Hartford, Connecticut ;

Kingscote dining room; and the William T. Lusk dining room. Is commissioned to decorate the White House for President Chester A. Arthur and Samuel Coleman's library, Newport, Rhode Island.

1883 L. C. Tiffany & Associated Artists disbands.

1884 Tiffany's first wife, Mary, dies on January 22nd.

1885 Forms the Tiffany Glass Company; decorates the Lyceum Theatre, New York; builds a mansion on 72nd Street and Madison Avenue, New York, in collaboration with architect Stanford White.

1886 Marries Louise Wakeman Knox on November 9th.

1888 Creates and installs the Kempner memorial window in Saint Paul's Episcopal Church, Milwaukee, Wisconsin (his largest figurative window)

1889 Travels throughout Europe; completes the Chittenden Window commission for Yale University, New Haven, Connecticut.

1890 Experiments with glass tiles; redecorates the Henry O. Havemeyer House, New York City.

1892 Forms the Tiffany Glass and Decorating Company; establishes the glass furnace at Corona on Long Island.

1893 Participates in the World's Columbian Exposition, Chicago, by exhibiting the Byzantine Chapel and other

William T. Lusk, New York; für die Bibliothek von Samuel Colman, Newport, Rhode Island; Präsident Chester A. Arthur beauftragt ihn mit der Innenausstattung einiger Räume des Weißen Hauses.

1883 L. C. Tiffany & Associated Artists wird aufgelöst.

1884 Tiffanys erste Frau, Mary, stirbt am 22. Januar.

1885 Gründet Tiffany Glass Company; übernimmt Innenausstattung des Lyceum Theatre, New York; baut mit dem Architekten Stanford White sein Stadthaus an der Ecke 72nd Street und Madison Avenue.

1886 9. Nov. Ehe mit seiner zweiten Frau, Louise Wakeman Knox.

1888 Führt das Kempner-Memorial-Fenster in der St. Paul's-Kathedrale in Milwaukee, Wisconsin, aus, das als sein größtes figuratives Fenster gilt.

1889 Bereist ganz Europa; stellt das Chittenden-Fenster für die Yale University in New Haven, Connecticut, fertig.

1890 Erste Experimente mit Glaskacheln; Neueinrichtung des Hauses von Henry O. Havemeyer in New York.

1892 Gründet die Tiffany Glass and Decorating Company sowie die Glashütte in Corona auf Long Island.

1893 Auf der Weltausstellung in Chicago zeigt er seine byzantinische Kapelle und liturgische Objekte sowie Fenster für öf-

pour la salle à manger de Kingscote, et celle de William T. Lusk ; reçoit une commande de décoration à la Maison Blanche pour le Président Chester A. Arthur et la bibliothèque de Samuel Coleman, à Newport, Rhode Island.

1883 L. C. Tiffany & Associated Artists est dissoute.

1884 Le 22 janvier, mort de Mary, la première épouse de Tiffany.

1885 Il crée la Tiffany Glass Company ; il décore le Lyceum Theatre, à New York ; il construit une résidence sur la 72e rue et Madison Avenue, à New York, en collaboration avec l'architecte Stanford White.

1886 Le 9 novembre, il épouse Louise Wakeman Knox.

1888 Il fabrique et installe le vitrail du Kempner Memorial dans l'église épiscopale Saint Paul, à Milwaukee, Wisconsin (le plus grand de ses vitraux figuratifs)

1889 Il voyage en Europe ; il exécute la commande de la Chittenden Window pour l'université de Yale, à New Haven, Connecticut.

1890 Il fait des essais de carreaux de verre ; il redécore la maison de Henry O. Havemeyer, à New York.

1892 Il fonde la Tiffany Glass and Decorating Company et il installe des hauts-fourneaux à Corona, Long Island.

1893 Il participe à la World's Columbian Exposition, à Chicago, où il présente la Chapelle Byzantine et d'autres

liturgical works as well as domestic windows; Tiffany Glass and Decorating Co. is awarded 54 medals at the exposition; begins production of Favrile glass at Corona factory.

1894 Tiffany registers the Favrile trademark at the U. S. Patent Office; exhibits glassware at the Salon of the Société Nationale des Beaux-Arts, Paris.

1894– Favrile glassware first sold.
1897 to the public; 53 pieces of Tiffany Favrile glassware are donated to the Metropolitan Museum of Art by Henry O. Havemeyer; 38 pieces of Favrile glassware sold to the Smithsonian Institution, Washington, D. C.; 23 pieces of Favrile glassware given to the Imperial Museum of Fine Arts, Tokyo.

1895 Exhibits stained glass windows in Paris executed by his firm from designs by Pierre Bonnard, Ker-Xavier Roussel, Maurice Denis, Henri de Toulouse-Lautrec, Paul Serusier, Felix Vallotton, and Edouard Vuillard among others.

1895– S. Bing's gallery "L'Art
1896 Nouveau" in Paris exhibits Favrile glassware and windows after Grasset and Serusier designs; commission for the decoration of the Pratt Institute Library in New York.

1897 Publishes list of completed Tiffany window commissions; establishes foundry and metal

fentliche und private Gebäude; Tiffany Glass & Decorating Company wird auf der Welt-ausstellung mit 54 Medaillen ausgezeichnet; in der Glas-hütte in Corona beginnt Pro-duktion von Favrile-Glas.

1894 Tiffany läßt beim US-Patent-amt das Warenzeichen »Favrile« registrieren; stellt im Salon der Société Nationale des Beaux-Arts in Paris Glasobjekte aus.

1894– Erster freier Verkauf von
1897 Favrile-Glasobjekten; Henry O. Havemeyer schenkt dem Metropolitan Museum of Art, New York, 53 Favrile-Glas-arbeiten; 38 Objekte werden von der Smithsonian Institu-tion in Washington, D. C., angekauft; dem Kaiserlichen Museum der Bildenden Künste in Tokio werden 23 Glasobjekte überreicht.

1895 In Paris werden nach Entwür-fen von Pierre Bonnard, Ker-Xavier Roussel, Maurice Denis, Henri de Toulouse-Lautrec, Paul Serusier, Felix Vallotton, Edouard Vuillard und anderen französischen Malern gefer-tigte Buntglasfenster ausgestellt.

1895– S. Bing stellt in seiner Pariser
1896 Galerie »L'Art Nouveau« Favrile-Glasobjekte und Fenster nach Entwürfen von Grasset und Se-rusier aus; Auftrag für die In-nenausstattung der Bibliothek des Pratt Institute, New York.

1897 Veröffentlicht vollständige Lis-te der von Tiffany ausgeführ-ten Fensteraufträge; erweitert

œuvres liturgiques, ainsi que des vitraux pour la maison ; à cette exposition, la Tiffany Glass and Decorating Co. se voit décerner 54 médailles ; l'usine de Corona commence à produire le verre Favrile.

1894 Tiffany fait enregistrer la marque Favrile au U. S. Patent Office ; il expose des verreries au Salon de la Société Nationale des Beaux-Arts, à Paris.

1894– Première vente au public
1897 de verre Favrile ; 53 pièces sont offertes en donation au Metropolitan Museum of Art, à New York, par Henry O. Havemeyer ; 38 autres pièces de Favrile sont vendues à la Smithsonian Institution de Washington, D. C. ; 23 sont offertes à l'Imperial Museum of Fine Arts, à Tokyo.

1895 A Paris, il expose des vitraux confectionnés par son entre-prise à partir de dessins, signés entre autres par Pierre Bonnard, Ker-Xavier Roussel, Maurice Denis, Henri de Toulouse-Lautrec, Paul Sérusier, Felix Vallotton et Edouard Vuillard.

1895– La galerie parisienne de S.
1896 Bing, « L'Art Nouveau », expose des verreries Favrile et des vitraux d'après Grasset et Serusier ; commande pour la décoration de la bibliothèque du Pratt Institute, à New York.

1897 Il publie la liste des vitraux commandés et exécutés ; il installe une fonderie et une

shop as part of expanded Corona factory; initiates production of lamps and desk sets.

1897–1898 Exhibits at the Salon de la Libre Esthétique, Brussels, Belgium.

1898 Opens showroom at 331–341 4th Avenue, New York; receives a commission from the Art Institute of Chicago.

1899 Exhibits windows, lamps and glassware at the Grafton Galleries, London; first documented production of the Butterfly and Nautilus lamps; Dragonfly lampshade design (attributed to Clara Driscoll) is created; production of enamelware begins.

1900 Participates in the Exposition Universelle, Paris, with more than 100 pieces of glassware, windows, lamps, mosaics, and enamels and is awarded several Grand Prizes by the jury; appointed Knight of the Legion of Honor by France; changes firm's name to Tiffany Studios; completes a commission for the Chicago Public Library.

1901 Participates in the Pan American Exposition, Buffalo, New York, and in the St. Petersburg, Russia, exposition of china; is awarded a Grand Prize at each; first Wisteria lamp is designed by Curtis Freschel.

1902 Is appointed design director of Tiffany & Co. after the death of his father, Charles

---

den Betrieb in Corona um eine Metallgießerei; nimmt die Produktion von Lampen und Schreibtischgarnituren auf.

1897–1898 Beteiligt sich am Salon de la Libre Esthétique in Brüssel, Belgien.

1898 Eröffnet Ausstellungsraum in der 4th Avenue 331–341, New York; Art Institute of Chicago gibt ein Glasfenster in Auftrag.

1899 Stellt in den Grafton Galleries in London Fenster, Lampen und Glasobjekte aus; die ersten bleiverglasten Lampenschirme entstehen: »Butterfly« und »Nautilus«; der Entwurf der »Dragonfly«-Lampe wird Clara Driscoll zugeschrieben; erste Emailarbeiten.

1900 Beteiligt sich mit über 100 Exponaten an der Weltausstellung in Paris: Glasobjekte, Fenster, Lampen, Mosaike und Emailarbeiten; wird mit mehreren Grand Prix und einer Goldmedaille ausgezeichnet und Chevalier de la Légion d'Honneur in Frankreich; benennt seine Firma in Tiffany Studios um; führt Auftrag für die Public Library in Chicago aus.

1901 Beteiligt sich an der Pan American Exposition in Buffalo, New York, an der Keramik-Ausstellung in St. Petersburg, Russland; wird bei beiden mit dem Grand Prix ausgezeichnet; Curtis Freschel entwirft erste Glyzinien-Lampe.

1902 Wird nach dem Tod seines Vaters Charles Lewis Tiffany künstlerischer Leiter von

---

forge au sein de l'usine de Corona qui s'agrandit ; il commence à produire des lampes et des ensembles de bureau.

1897–1898 Il expose au Salon de la Libre Esthétique à Bruxelles en Belgique.

1898 Il ouvre un magasin d'exposition aux 331–341 4th Avenue, à New York ; il reçoit une commande de l'Art Institute de Chicago.

1899 Il expose vitraux, lampes et verreries aux Grafton Galleries, à Londres ; première production connue de lampes « Papillon » et « Nautile » ; création du modèle d'abat-jour « Libellule » (attribué à Clara Driscoll) ; il se lance dans la production d'émaux.

1900 Il participe à l'Exposition Universelle de Paris, avec plus de cent pièces de verreries, vitraux, lampes, mosaïques et émaux ; il reçoit plusieurs Grands Prix du jury ; la France le nomme Chevalier de la Légion d'Honneur ; il change le nom de sa société pour celui de Tiffany Studios ; il achève une commande pour la Chicago Public Library.

1901 Il participe à la Pan American Exposition, à Buffalo, New York, et à l'exposition de céramique à St. Petersbourg en Russie ; il reçoit un Grand Prix dans ces deux villes ; la première lampe « Glycine » est dessinée par Curtis Freschel.

1902 Après le décès de son père, Charles Lewis Tiffany, il est nommé directeur artistique de

Lewis Tiffany; takes part in the Turin World Exposition, Italy and is awarded the Grand Prize for his *Lily-Cluster* lamp; forms Tiffany Furnaces but retains Tiffany Studios name for work produced at the Corona factory.

1902–1904	Constructs Laurelton Hall, his summer home, near Oyster Bay on the north shore of Long Island.
1904	Second wife, Louise, dies May 9; exhibits at the St. Louis International Exposition; begins designing jewelry.
1905	Exhibits at the Salon of the Société des Artistes Français, Paris.
1906	Publishes a Tiffany Studios price list with model numbers for lampshades, bases, candlesticks, and desk sets.
1911	Completes a glass-mosaic curtain for the National Theater in Mexico City.
1912–1914	Constructs mosaic murals and domes for the Roman Catholic cathedral in St. Louis, Missouri, with thirty million pieces of glass mosaic.
1913	Publishes an updated version of the 1906 Tiffany Studios price list and includes new models since 1906; visits Nuremberg, Germany, and Havana, Cuba, to oversee window commissions; holds an Egyptian Fête at the Tiffany Studios showroom.

Tiffany & Co.; beteiligt sich an der Weltausstellung in Turin in Italien; wird für das Lampenmodell »Lily Cluster« mit einem Grand Prix ausgezeichnet; gründet Tiffany Furnaces, behält aber den Namen Tiffany Studios für in Corona gefertigte Objekte bei.

1902–1904	An der Oyster Bay an der Nordküste von Long Island entsteht seine Sommerresidenz Laurelton Hall.
1904	Am 9. Mai Tod seiner zweiten Frau, Louise; nimmt an der Weltausstellung in St. Louis teil; beginnt mit eigenen Schmuckentwürfen.
1905	Beteiligt sich am Salon der Société des Artistes Français in Paris.
1906	Veröffentlicht Preisliste der Tiffany Studios mit Modellnummern für Lampenschirme, -füße, Kerzenhalter und Schreibtischgarnituren.
1911	Fertigung eines Glasmosaikvorhangs für das Nationaltheater in Mexiko-Stadt.
1912–1914	Für die römisch-katholische Kathedrale in St. Louis, Missouri, entstehen Wand- und Kuppelmosaiken aus insgesamt über 30 Millionen Glassteinen.
1913	Veröffentlicht eine aktualisierte Version seiner 1906 erstmals erschienenen Preisliste für Lampenschirme und -füße; reist nach Nürnberg und nach Havanna, Kuba, um die Installation von Glasfenstern zu überwachen; »Ägyptisches Fest« in den Tiffany Studios.

Tiffany & Co. ; il participe à l'Exposition mondiale de Turin où il reçoit le grand prix pour sa lampe « Bouquet de fleurs de lys » ; il fonde les Hauts-Fourneaux Tiffany, mais conserve le nom de Tiffany Studios pour les œuvres produites à l'usine de Corona.

1902–1904	Il fait construire Laurelton Hall, sa résidence d'été, près de Oyster Bay sur la rive nord de Long Island.
1904	Le 9 mai, mort de sa seconde épouse, Louise ; il participe à l'Exposition Internationale de Saint Louis et commence à dessiner des bijoux.
1905	Il expose au Salon de la Société des Artistes Français, à Paris.
1906	Il publie un catalogue de tarifs des Tiffany Studios comportant les modèles d'abat-jour, de pieds de lampes, de chandeliers et d'ensembles de bureau.
1911	Il achève un rideau en mosaïque de verre pour le National Theater de Mexico.
1912–1914	Il fabrique des fresques et des coupoles de mosaïque pour la cathédrale catholique de Saint Louis, à Missouri, où il utilise 30 millions de morceaux de verre.
1913	Il publie une mise à jour du premier catalogue des Tiffany Studios en ajoutant les nouveaux modèles créés depuis 1906 ; il se rend à Nuremberg, en Allemagne, et à La Havane, à Cuba, pour superviser des commandes de vitraux ; « Fête égyptienne » aux Tiffany Studios.

1914	Charles de Kay publishes Tiffany's biography in an edition of 492 copies; an additional 10 copies are printed on vellum with cover design by L. C. Tiffany; installs The Bathers window, originally commissioned by Captain J. R. De Lamar around 1912, at Laurelton Hall.	**1914**	Charles De Kay veröffentlicht »The Art Work of Louis C. Tiffany« in einer Auflage von 492 und zehn weiteren auf Pergament gedruckten Exemplaren mit einem von Tiffany gestalteten Einband; das um 1912 von Captain De Lamar bestellte Fenster »The Bathers« wird in Laurelton Hall installiert.	**1914**	Charles de Kay fait paraître une biographie de Tiffany en 492 exemplaires ; 10 autres exemplaires sont imprimés sur vélin en couverture des dessins de L. C. Tiffany ; il installe le vitrail de « La Baignade », commandé à l'origine par le Capitaine J. R. De Lamar vers 1912, à Laurelton Hall.
1915	Participates in the Pan-Pacific Exposition, San Francisco, California; executes The Dream Garden mosaic mural after design by Maxfield Parrish for the lobby of the Curtis Publishing Company building in Philadelphia.	**1915**	Nimmt an der Pan-Pacific Exposition in San Francisco teil; das von Maxfield Parrish entworfene Wandmosaik »The Dream Garden« für die Lobby des Gebäudes der Curtis Publishing Company in Philadelphia wird fertiggestellt.	**1915**	Il participe à la Pan-Pacific Exposition de San Francisco, Californie ; il réalise le « Jardin de rêve », fresque de mosaïque à partir de dessins de Maxfield Parrish, pour le vestibule du siège social de la Curtis Publishing Company à Philadelphie.
1916	Retrospective of Tiffany's work and «The Quest of Beauty" theme-party held at the Tiffany Studios showroom to celebrate his 68th birthday; mosaic chapel from the 1893 Columbian Exposition in Chicago, previously installed in 1899 at the Cathedral of St. John the Divine in New York, is removed, restored and reinstalled at Laurelton Hall; visits Alaska.	**1916**	Anläßlich seines 68. Geburtstags Retrospektive von Tiffanys Werk und »Quest-of-Beauty«-Themenfeier in Ausstellungsräumen der Tiffany Studios in der Madison Avenue; die Kapelle der Chicagoer Weltausstellung 1893, 1899 in die St.-John-the-Divine-Kathedrale, New York, integriert, wird dort entfernt, restauriert und auf dem Gelände von Laurelton Hall aufgebaut; Reise nach Alaska.	**1916**	Rétrospective de l'œuvre de Tiffany et soirée « Quête de la Beauté » dans les salons d'exposition des Tiffany Studios pour la célébration de son 68ème anniversaire ; la chapelle de l'Exposition Colombienne de Chicago, en 1893, installée depuis 1899 à la cathédrale de Saint John the Divine à New York, est démontée, restaurée, et réinstallée à Laurelton Hall ; Tiffany visite l'Alaska.
1918	Establishes the Louis Comfort Tiffany Foundation to aid gifted young artists.	**1918**	Gründet Louis Comfort Tiffany Foundation zur Unterstützung begabter junger Künstler.	**1918**	Il crée la Fondation Louis Comfort Tiffany pour venir en aide aux jeunes artistes de talent.
1919	Retires; divides his Tiffany Studios into Tiffany Furnaces, managed by A. Douglas Nash, to produce Favrile glassware, and the Tiffany Ecclesiastical Department to produce windows, mosaics, lamps, etc.	**1919**	Zieht sich zurück; Tiffany Studios aufgeteilt in die Glasmanufaktur unter A. Douglas Nash (Tiffany Furnaces Inc.), die Favrile-Glas produziert, und das Tiffany Ecclesiastical Department für Glasfenster, Mosaiken und bleiverglaste Lampen.	**1919**	Il prend sa retraite ; il divise ses Tiffany Studios en Hauts-Fourneaux Tiffany, dirigés par A. Douglas Nash, destinés à la production du verre Favrile, et en Département liturgique Tiffany, pour la production des vitraux, lampes, mosaïques, etc.
1922	Creates the Te Deum Laudamus mosaic triptych for the First	**1922**	Entwirft das Mosaiktriptychon »Te Deum Laudamus« für die	**1922**	Réalise le triptyque de mosaïque « Te Deum Laudamus » pour la

	United Methodist Church, Los Angeles, California.		First United Methodist Church in Los Angeles, Kalifornien.		First United Methodist Church de Los Angeles, Californie.
1924	L. C. Tiffany Furnaces dissolves.	1924	Glashütte in Corona wird geschlossen.	1924	Dissolution des Hauts-Fourneaux L. C. Tiffany.
1927	Andrew Dickson White Museum at Cornell University, Ithaca, New York, is given a collection of Tiffany glass.	1927	Andrew Dickson White Museum der Cornell University, Ithaca, New York, erhält Sammlung von Tiffany-Gläsern.	1927	Le Andrew Dickson White Museum de la Cornell University, à Ithaca, New York, reçoit une collection de verreries Tiffany.
1932	Tiffany Studios declares bankruptcy.	1932	Tiffany Studios melden Konkurs an.	1932	Mise en faillite des Tiffany Studios.
1933	Louis Comfort Tiffany dies on January 17; Westminster Memorial Studios is created by former employees to complete outstanding Tiffany Studios commissions.	1933	Louis Comfort Tiffany stirbt am 17. Januar in New York; ehemalige Mitarbeiter der Tiffany Studios gründen Westminster Memorial Studios, um offene Aufträge auszuführen.	1933	Le 17 janvier, mort de Louis Comfort Tiffany ; d'anciens employés fondent les Westminster Memorial Studios pour réaliser les commandes restantes des Tiffany Studios.
1934	First of several auctions liquidates the firm's inventory.	1934	Erste von mehreren Auktionen zur Liquidierung des Firmeninventars.	1934	Une première vente aux enchères liquide l'inventaire de l'entreprise.
1946	Contents of Laurelton Hall are sold at public auction in New York.	1946	Die Einrichtung von Laurelton Hall wird in New York öffentlich versteigert.	1946	Mise aux enchères des biens appartenant au Laurelton Hall, à New York.
1957	Laurelton Hall is partially destroyed by fire.	1957	Laurelton Hall durch einen Brand teilweise zerstört.	1957	Laurelton Hall en partie détruit par un incendie.
1958	First important retrospective exhibition of Tiffany's work is held at the Museum of Contemporary Crafts in New York.	1958	Das Museum of Contemporary Crafts, New York, zeigt erste bedeutende Tiffany-Retrospektive.	1958	Première rétrospective importante de l'œuvre de Tiffany, au Museum of Contemporary Crafts, à New York.
1967	Heckscher Museum in Huntington, New York, exhibits Tiffany's work.	1967	Tiffany-Ausstellung im Heckscher Museum, Huntington, New York.	1967	Exposition de l'œuvre de Tiffany au Heckscher Museum de Huntington, New York.
1979	Tiffany's paintings exhibited at the Grey Art Gallery, New York University, New York.	1979	Die Grey Art Gallery der New York University zeigt Gemälde von Tiffany.	1979	Les peintures de Tiffany sont exposées à la Grey Art Gallery, New York University.
1989– 1990	"Masterworks of Louis Comfort Tiffany" presented at the Smithsonian Institution, Washington, D. C., and the Metropolitan Museum of Art, New York.	1989– 1990	Ausstellung »Masterworks of Louis Comfort Tiffany« in der Smithsonian Institution, Washington, D. C., und im Metropolitan Museum of Art, New York.	1989– 1990	Présentation de « Chefs-d'œuvre de Louis Comfort Tiffany » à la Smithsonian Institution, à Washington, D. C., et au Metropolitan Museum of Art, New York.
1991	"Masterworks of Louis Comfort Tiffany" held in Japan; exhibition travels to Tokyo, Kobe, Nagoya, and Toyama.	1991	»Masterworks of Louis Comfort Tiffany« als Wanderausstellung in Japan: in Tokio, Kobe, Nagoya und Toyama.	1991	Présentation de « Chefs-d'œuvre de Louis Comfort Tiffany » au Japon: à Tokyo, Kobe, Nagoya, et Toyama.

1993	Major exhibition of the Neustadt Collection of Tiffany lamps held at the University of Miami, Florida.	1993	Große Ausstellung von Tiffany-Lampen der Sammlung Neustadt an der University of Miami, Florida.	1993	Grande exposition de la Neustadt Collection de lampes Tiffany à l'université de Miami, en Floride.
1997	Christie's auction house in New York sells a Tiffany *Lotus* lamp for nearly $2.9 million.	1997	Das Auktionshaus Christie's in New York versteigert eine »Lotus«-Lampe von Tiffany für fast 2,9 Millionen Dollar.	1997	La maison Christie's, à New York, vend une lampe « Lotus » de Tiffany pour presque $2.9 millions.
1997–1999	Tiffany's Byzantine Chapel is reassembled and restored at the instigation of his grandson-in-law; reopens at the Charles Hosmer Morse Museum, Winter Park, Florida	1997–1999	Tiffanys byzantinische Kapelle wird auf Initiative des Mannes seiner Enkelin wieder aufgebaut, restauriert und im Charles Hosmer Morse Museum, Winterpark, Florida, neu eröffnet	1997–1999	La Chapelle Byzantine de Tiffany est remontée et restaurée à l'instigation de son petit-fils par alliance ; elle est récouverte au Charles Hosmer Morse Museum, à Winter Park, en Floride

Bibliography　　Bibliographie

Amaya, Mario. *Tiffany Glass*. New York: Walker and Sons, 1966.

Bing, Samuel; Koch, Robert. *Artistic America. Tiffany Glass, and Art Nouveau*. Cambridge, MA: The Massachusetts Institute of Technology, 1970.

Constantino, Maria. *Art Nouveau*. London: Pre-Publishing, 1999.

Couldrey, Vivienne. *The Art of Louis Comfort Tiffany*. The Weilfleet Press, 1989.

DeKay, Charles. *The Art Work of Louis C. Tiffany*. Garden City, NJ: Doubleday, Page & Co., 1914.

DeKay, Charles. *The Art Work of Louis C. Tiffany*. 2nd ed. New York, NY: Apollo, 1987.

Doros, Paul E. *The Tiffany Collection of the Chrysler Museum at Norfolk*. Norfolk, VA: Chrysler Museum, 1978.

Duncan, Alastair. *Fin de Siècle*. New York: Abbeville Press, 1989.

Duncan, Alastair. *Louis Comfort Tiffany*. New York: Harry N. Abrams, Inc., 1992.

Duncan, Alastair. *Tiffany at Auction*. New York: Rizzoli, 1981.

Duncan, Alastair. *Tiffany Windows*. New York: Simon and Schuster, 1980.

Duncan, Alastair; Eidelberg, Martin and Harris, Neal. *Masterworks of Louis Comfort Tiffany*. New York: Harry N. Abrams, Inc., 1989.

Duncan, Alastair and Yoshimizu, Tsuneo. *Masterworks of Louis Comfort Tiffany*. Tokio: Tokyo Metropolitan Teien Art Museum, 1991.

Duncan, Alastair et al. *The World of Louis Comfort Tiffany: A Selection from the Anchorman Collection*. Japan: Greco Corporation Fine Art Department, 1994.

Feldstein, William J. Jr. and Duncan, Alastair. *The Lamps of Tiffany Studios*. New York: Harry N. Abrams, 1982.

Freilinghuysen, Alice Cooney. *Louis Comfort Tiffany at the Metropolitan Museum*. New York: Metropolitan Museum of Art, 1998.

Greenhalgh, Paul, ed. *Art Nouveau 1890–1914*. London: Victoria and Albert Museum in association with the National Gallery of Art, Washington, D. C., 2000.

Isham, Samuel. *The History of American Painting*. New York: MacMillan, 1905.

Joppein, Rüdiger et al. *Louis C. Tiffany. Meisterwerke des amerikanischen Jugendstils*. Hamburg: Museum für Kunst und Gewerbe Hamburg, 1999.

Koch, Robert. *Louis Comfort Tiffany 1848–1933*. New York: Museum of Contemporary Crafts of the American Craftmen's Council, 1958.

Koch, Robert. *Louis C. Tiffany – Rebel in Glass*. 3rd ed. New York: Crown Publishers, 1982.

Koch, Robert. *S. Bing, Artistic America, Tiffany Glass and Art Nouveau*. Cambridge, MA: Publishing Company, 1970.

Koch, Robert. *Tiffany's Glass, Bronzes, Lamps*. New York: Crown Publishers, 1971.

The Lamps of Tiffany: Highlights of Egon and Hildegard Neustadt Collection. Exhibition catalogue. Miami: University of Miami Press, 1993.

Lewis, Arnold; Turner, James and McQuillen, Steven. *The Opulent Interiors of the Gilded Age: All 203 Photographs from the "Artistic House."* New York: Dover Publications Inc., 1897.

Louis C. Tiffany. Galerie Art Focus, Collection Max Kohler. Zürich, 1997.

Louis C. Tiffany. Meisterwerke des amerikanischen Jugendstils. Köln: DuMont, 1999.

McKean, Hugh. *The "Lost" Treasures of Louis Comfort Tiffany*. New York: Doubleday & Co., 1980.

McKean, Hugh. *Louis Comfort Tiffany* (in German). Weingarten, Germany: Weingarten, 1988.

McKean, Hugh. *"The Lovely Riddle": Reflections on Art*. Winterpark, FL: Charles Hosmer Morse Foundation, Inc., 1997.

McKean, Hugh. *Tiffany's Chapel – A Treasure Rediscovered*. Winterpark, FL: Charles Hosmer Morse Foundation, Inc., 1993.

McKean, Hugh. *Treasures of Tiffany*. Exhibition catalogue. Chicago: Museum of Science and Industry, 1982.

Neustadt, Egon. *The Lamps of Tiffany*. New York: The Fairchild Press, 1970.

Objects of Art of Three Continents and Antique Oriental Rugs: The Extensive Collection Louis Comfort Tiffany Foundation. New York: Parke-Bernet Galleries, Inc., 1946.

Paton, James. *Lamps. A Collector's Guide*. New York: Charles Scribner's Sons, 1978.

Porter, Norman and Jackson, Douglas. *Tiffany*. London: Octopus, 1988.

Porter, Norman and Jackson, Douglas. *Tiffany Glassware*. New York: Crown Publishers, 1988.

Price, Joan Elliott. "*Louis Comfort Tiffany. The Painting Career of a Colorist*." American University Studies, Vol. 28, 1996.

Proddow, Penny and Healy, Debra. *Tiffany et les joalliers américains*. Photographies by David Behl. Paris: Editions Vito, 1987.

Purtell, Joseph. *The Tiffany Touch*. Kingsport, TN: Kingsport Press, 1971.

Revi, Albert Christian. *American Art Nouveau Glass*. New York: Thomas Nelson & Sons, 1968.

Selz, Peter. *Art Nouveau*. Exhibition catalogue. New York: Museum of Modern Art, 1960.

Speenburgh, Gertrude. *The Arts of the Tiffanys*. Chicago: Lightner, 1956.

Spillman, Jane Shadel. *Glass from World's Fairs: 1851–1904*. Corning, NY: Corning Museum of Glass, 1988.

Steeg, Moise S. Jr. *Tiffany Favril Art Glass*. London: Schiffer Publishing Ltd., 1997.

Stoddards, William O. *The Tiffanys of America: History and Genealogy*. New York: Nelson Otis Tiffany Publisher, 1901.

Syford, Ethel. *Examples of Recent Works from the Studio of Louis C. Tiffany*. 1911.

Tessa, Paul. *L'art de Louis Tiffany*. Adaptation française de Philippe Plumecoq. Paris: Editions Soline, 1990.

Tessa, Paul. *The Art of Louis Comfort Tiffany*. London: Quintet, 1988.

Tiffany, Louis C. "*American Art Supreme in Colored Glass*." The Forum 15 (1893): pp. 621–628.

Tiffany, Louis C. "*Color and its Kinship to Sound*." The Art World 2 (1917): pp. 142–143.

Tiffany, Louis C. "*The Gospel of Good Taste*." Country Life in America 19 (November 1910): p. 105.

Tiffany, Louis C. "*The Quest of Beauty*." Harper's Bazaar (December 1917): pp. 43–44.

Tiffany, Louis C. "*What Is the Quest of Beauty?*" International Studio 58 (April 1916): p. lxiii.

Tiffany. Florence: Rizzoli, 1979.

Tiffany: Innovation in American Design. New York: Christie's, 1999.

Tiffany Studios. *Bronze Lamps*. New York: Frank Presbrey Co., 1904.

Tiffany Studios. *A Partial List of Windows*. New York: Frank Presbrey Co., 1910.

Tiffany Studios. *Tiffany Favrile Glass*. New York: Frank Presbrey Co., 1905.

Tiffany Studios. *Tiffany Favrile Glass Made under the Supervision of Mr. Louis C. Tiffany*. New York: Frank Presbrey Co., 1899.

Tiffany's Tiffany. Exhibition catalogue. Corning, NY: Corning Museum of Art, 1980.

Weisberg, Gabriel P. *Art Nouveau Bing: Paris Style 1900*. New York: Harry N. Abrams, Inc., 1986.

Wheeler, Candace. *Yesterday in a Busy Life*. New York: Harper and Brothers, 1918.

Wilie, Elizabeth and Cheek, Sheldon. *The Art of Stained and Decorative Glass*. Todtri, 1997.

Zapata, Janet. *The Jewelry and Enamels of Louis Comfort Tiffany*. London: Thames and Hudson, 1993.

© 2004 TASCHEN GmbH
Hohenzollernring 53, D–50672 Köln
www.taschen.com

Edited by Simone Philippi, Cologne
Editorial coordination: Agents – Producers – Editors, Overath
German translation: Wolfgang Himmelberg, Düsseldorf
French translation: Simone Manceau, Paris

Cover design: Angelika Taschen, Cologne
Design: Claudia Frey, Cologne
Production coordination: Ute Wachendorf, Cologne

ISBN 0–681–16584–7
Printed in China